Israel's Sacrificial System

Atonement and Redemption

Israel's Sacrificial System

Atonement and Redemption

Vinu V Das

Tabor Press

© 2025 Tabor Press. All rights reserved. No part of this publication may be reproduced, distributed, or transmitted in any form or by any means without the prior written permission of the publisher, except in the case of brief quotations embodied in critical reviews and certain other noncommercial uses permitted by copyright law.

ISBN: 978-1-997541-01-1

Table of Contents

CHAPTER 1: THE FIRST SACRIFICES IN THE BIBLE 10

    Section 1: The Sacrifice of Abel vs. Cain 11

    Section 2: Noah's Burnt Offering After the Flood 13

    Section 3: Abraham's Test – The Near-Sacrifice of Isaac 14

    Section 4: The First Passover Sacrifice 16

    Conclusion 18

CHAPTER 2: THE BURNT OFFERING (OLAH) 19

    Section 1: Old Testament Background of the Burnt Offering 20

    Section 2: Procedure of the Burnt Offering 21

    Section 3: Purpose of the Burnt Offering 25

    Section 4: Significance for Israel's Worship and Beyond 27

    Conclusion 28

CHAPTER 3: THE GRAIN OFFERING (MINCHAH) 30

    Section 1: Biblical Basis for the Grain Offering 31

    Section 2: Procedure for Presenting the Grain Offering.. 32

    Section 3: Ingredients and Their Symbolism 34

    Section 4: Purpose of the Grain Offering 36

    Section 5: Theological Significance 38

    Section 6: Practical Reflections and Contemporary Relevance 40

    Conclusion 42

CHAPTER 4: THE PEACE OFFERING (SHELAMIM) ... 43

Section 1: Biblical Basis and Terminology 43

Section 2: Different Types of Peace Offerings 45

Section 3: Procedure and Distribution of the Peace Offering 46

Section 4: Purpose and Significance of the Peace Offering 49

Section 5: The Social and Theological Dimensions of Shelamim 50

Section 6: Lasting Lessons and Contemporary Reflection 52

Conclusion 53

CHAPTER 5: THE SIN OFFERING (CHATAT) 55

Section 1: Biblical Context and Terminology 56

Section 2: Purpose of the Sin Offering 57

Section 3: Detailed Procedure of the Sin Offering 58

Section 4: Distinguishing the Sin Offering from the Guilt Offering 61

Section 5: Theological Significance of the Sin Offering 62

Section 6: Broader Reflections and Contemporary Relevance 63

Conclusion 65

CHAPTER 6: THE GUILT OFFERING (ASHAM) 66

Section 1: Biblical Context and Key Passages 66

Section 2: Core Purpose of the Guilt Offering 68

Section 3: Procedure of the Guilt Offering 69

Section 4: Distinguishing the Guilt Offering from the Sin Offering 71

Section 5: Theological Significance of the Guilt Offering 72

Conclusion 74

CHAPTER 7: THE RED HEIFER SACRIFICE 76

Section 1: Biblical Context and Overview 76

Section 2: The Heifer and Its Preparation 78

Section 3: The Purification Process 80

Section 4: Purpose and Theological Significance 81

Section 5: Practical and Ritual Implications in Ancient Israel 83

Conclusion 84

CHAPTER 8: THE TWO GOATS OF YOM KIPPUR (DAY OF ATONEMENT) 86

Section 1: Scriptural Foundations in Leviticus 16 87

Section 2: Preparation of the High Priest 87

Section 3: Offering the Bull for the High Priest's Atonement 89

Section 4: The Goat "for the Lord" 90

Section 5: The Goat "for Azazel" 91

Section 6: The Holiness of Yom Kippur 93

Section 7: Symbolic and Theological Dimensions 95

Section 8: Additional Rituals and Considerations 96

Section 9: Yom Kippur in Israel's Spiritual Life 97

Section 10: Contemporary Reflections and Lessons 98

Conclusion 99

CHAPTER 9: OTHER SACRIFICES AND OFFERINGS 101

Section 1: Drink Offerings 101

Section 2: Wave and Heave Offerings 103

Section 3: Firstfruits Offerings 105

Section 4: Tithe Offerings 106

Section 5: Lesser-Noted and Occasional Offerings 108

Section 6: Integration of Everyday Life and Worship 110

Section 7: Theological Reflections and Contemporary Lessons 110

Conclusion 112

CHAPTER 10: THE END OF THE OLD TESTAMENT SACRIFICES 113

Section 1: The Destruction of the Second Temple (70 CE) 114

Section 2: Prophetic and Theological Undercurrents 115

Section 3: Emergence of Rabbinic Judaism 116

Section 4: Perspectives from the Early Christian Movement 117

Section 5: Lasting Effects on Jewish Worship and Identity 118

Section 6: Biblical Reflections on the Temple's Destruction 120

Section 7: Implications for Modern Worship and Study 121

Conclusion 122

CHAPTER 11: JESUS CHRIST – THE ULTIMATE SACRIFICE 124

Section 1: Jesus as the "Lamb of God" 125

Section 2: The Cross as the Fulfillment of Old Testament Sacrifices 127

Section 3: The Once-for-All Sacrifice 130

Section 4: No More Need for Animal Sacrifices 132

Section 5: The Cross and Resurrection: Victory Over Sin and Death 134

Section 6: The Eucharist / Lord's Supper as a New Covenant Memorial 135

Section 7: Ongoing Implications for Christian Life and Worship 137

Conclusion 138

CHAPTER 1: THE FIRST SACRIFICES IN THE BIBLE

Sacrifice is one of the earliest themes we encounter in the biblical narrative. Long before the detailed instructions of Leviticus or the construction of the Tabernacle, human beings offered gifts to God in recognition of His authority, out of gratitude, or as an appeal for forgiveness and favor. These inaugural sacrifices lay the foundation for understanding the broader sacrificial system that would develop in the history of Israel. Equally important, they foreshadow the ultimate sacrifice of Christ in the New Testament, although the full revelation of that comes much later.

In this chapter, we will examine four key sacrificial moments in the earliest books of the Bible. First, we will look at the conflicting sacrifices of two brothers—Cain and Abel—in the

Genesis account and what this story reveals about worship and the condition of the human heart. Next, we will turn to Noah's burnt offering after the great Flood, observing how sacrifice often marked new beginnings and covenants in Scripture. We will then consider the test of Abraham, who was called to offer up his son Isaac, an event that has long prompted discussions about faith, obedience, and the nature of God's redemptive plan. Finally, we will explore the first Passover sacrifice in the Book of Exodus, a foundational event for Israel's identity and an enduring reminder of God's saving power.

Section 1: The Sacrifice of Abel vs. Cain

The first explicit mention of sacrifices offered by human beings appears soon after humanity's expulsion from the Garden of Eden. Genesis 4:1–7 records that Adam and Eve had two sons: Cain, a farmer, and Abel, a shepherd. In the course of time, both brothers brought an offering to the Lord. Cain offered "some of the fruits of the soil" (Genesis 4:3), while Abel brought "fat portions from some of the firstborn of his flock" (Genesis 4:4).

What unfolds in the text is a surprising divergence in how God receives their offerings. We read that the Lord looked favorably toward Abel's offering but did not favor Cain's. This difference led Cain to become "very angry," which ultimately escalated into jealousy and murder (Genesis 4:5–8). At first glance, the passage raises the question: *Why was Abel's offering accepted while Cain's was not?*

Biblical interpreters have offered several perspectives. One view emphasizes the nature or quality of the offering. Abel brought the very best—"fat portions from the firstborn"—

demonstrating his reverence and gratitude. By contrast, the text seems to imply that Cain's offering may have been perfunctory or lacking devotion. Another perspective focuses on the attitude of the worshipper. In Hebrews 11:4, the New Testament reflects on this incident, stating that "By faith Abel brought God a better offering than Cain did," underscoring that Abel's faith, rather than merely the material quality of his offering, was the key difference.

Additionally, scholars note that God's response is pastoral before it is punitive. He urges Cain to master his anger, warning that "sin is crouching at your door; it desires to have you, but you must rule over it" (Genesis 4:7). This exhortation suggests that Cain's heart posture—his resentment, envy, or disobedience—was already an issue before he committed the act of murder. The sacrifice itself becomes a sort of litmus test, revealing the true spiritual condition of each brother.

Within Christian theology, many interpret Abel's sacrifice as a foreshadowing of the faith-based sacrificial system to come, wherein the worshipper's trust in God matters even more than the external gift. While the actual content of each brother's sacrifice (animal vs. produce) is important to the narrative, the real lesson lies in recognizing that the authenticity of one's devotion and the faith behind the offering are primary.

In later passages, such as 1 John 3:12, Cain is portrayed as one who "belonged to the evil one," highlighting the moral dimension of the story. Abel, on the other hand, is lauded for his righteousness. Thus, these earliest sacrifices illustrate that worship is not merely about ritual but about a sincere heart. This principle resonates throughout Scripture, culminating in the New Testament teachings that the sacrifice God desires is a "broken spirit; a broken and contrite heart" (Psalm 51:17).

Section 2: Noah's Burnt Offering After the Flood

Some centuries after Cain and Abel, humanity spiraled into widespread corruption, prompting the judgment of the global Flood. One of the most significant transitions in biblical history occurs when Noah, preserved by God in the ark, emerges onto dry land. According to Genesis 8:20–21, Noah's immediate response was to build an altar and offer burnt offerings of every clean animal and bird. This moment is critical for several reasons, marking a new beginning for humanity and illustrating how sacrifice is intertwined with thanksgiving and covenant renewal.

Burnt offerings (often called *olah* in Hebrew) involve the entire sacrifice being consumed by fire on the altar. The aroma was said to be "pleasing" or "soothing" to the Lord (Genesis 8:21), language that indicates acceptance and delight in the worshipper's act. While the narrative does not provide extensive detail regarding the procedure of this specific sacrifice, later passages in Exodus and Leviticus clarify that the entire animal was typically given over to God, symbolizing complete devotion and surrender. In Noah's case, this was an act of gratitude and humility in response to God's mercy, since he and his family were the only survivors of the Flood.

Following this act of worship, God makes a covenantal promise: never again will He curse the ground because of human sin, nor will He destroy all living creatures as He had done (Genesis 8:21–22). Thus, the sacrifice and the blessing are closely linked. Noah's offering reflects the principle that sacrifice can be a gesture of thanksgiving and a plea for divine grace to guide the future. The gift is not meant to manipulate God but to acknowledge dependence and reverence.

Theologically, Noah's sacrifice also underscores the idea that God preserves a remnant and ushers in new phases of salvation history through acts of grace. Noah's burnt offering is among the first clear examples of a whole burnt offering, prefiguring later sacrifices in Israel's worship, wherein the entire animal would be dedicated to God. It hints at the totality of surrender that defines authentic worship: the worshipper does not simply make a token gesture but places everything on the altar.

Given that the text emphasizes God's pleasure at the aroma of the offering, the story also demonstrates the power of genuine worship to restore a sense of fellowship between God and humankind. While the curses and the memory of human evil remain realities, Noah's immediate sacrificial response allows him to move forward under a renewed blessing. In Christian reflection, this moment points us forward to the need for ultimate redemption—something beyond repeated burnt offerings. Yet it remains significant as an archetype of worship born out of deliverance and gratitude.

Section 3: Abraham's Test – The Near-Sacrifice of Isaac

Perhaps one of the most poignant and theologically profound sacrificial narratives in the Bible is found in Genesis 22, where Abraham is asked by God to sacrifice his son Isaac. Referred to in Jewish tradition as the *Akedah* (the Binding of Isaac), this tests Abraham's faith at the highest level.

The story begins with a stark command: "Take your son, your only son, whom you love—Isaac—and go to the region of

Moriah. Sacrifice him there as a burnt offering" (Genesis 22:2). Isaac was the child of the promise, the son through whom God had declared Abraham would have countless descendants (Genesis 17:19). Therefore, the command to sacrifice Isaac appears to contradict God's own covenantal pledge.

From a theological perspective, this dilemma highlights the tension between obedience and promise, faith and reason. Abraham proceeds in obedience, journeying to the place God shows him. Along the way, he prophesies in faith that "God himself will provide the lamb" (Genesis 22:8). This statement becomes key not only to the resolution of the story but to later Christian interpretation, as it resonates with the idea that God ultimately provides the sacrifice necessary for atonement.

Just as Abraham is about to slay his son, an angel of the Lord intervenes, stopping him and affirming that Abraham's devotion has been demonstrated. Instead, Abraham sees a ram caught in a thicket, which he sacrifices in Isaac's stead (Genesis 22:13). Abraham names the place "The Lord Will Provide" (Genesis 22:14), and God repeats His promise of blessing and numerous descendants.

The significance of this event is profound. Firstly, it establishes Abraham's extraordinary faith: he trusted that God's promise would stand even if obedience to God's immediate command seemed to threaten that very promise (Hebrews 11:17–19). Secondly, it foreshadows the concept of substitutionary atonement. Isaac, the intended sacrifice, is spared through the provision of a ram. Christian exegetes draw a parallel to Jesus Christ, who is similarly referred to as the Lamb of God provided by the Father on behalf of sinners (John 1:29).

Unlike the other sacrificial moments in this chapter, Abraham's test does not simply revolve around gratitude or atonement for sin; rather, it highlights the radical obedience of the faithful and the absolute sovereignty of God over life itself. It also sets in place a trajectory that sacrifices are never about human will or whim; they proceed from divine command and provision. If Cain and Abel's account underlines the state of the human heart and Noah's offering shows gratitude for deliverance, Abraham's near-sacrifice of Isaac reveals the ultimate act of surrender—trusting God even with the future of the covenant family.

Section 4: The First Passover Sacrifice

Moving forward in the biblical timeline, the descendants of Abraham—now numerous—found themselves enslaved in Egypt. The Book of Exodus recounts the confrontation between Moses and Pharaoh, culminating in a series of plagues that God sent against the Egyptians. The final plague, the death of the firstborn, set the stage for the first Passover sacrifice, which would become a cornerstone of Israel's religious identity.

In Exodus 12:1–14, God instructs the Israelites to select an unblemished lamb on the tenth day of the first month, slaughter it at twilight on the fourteenth day, and place some of its blood on the doorframes of their houses. That very night, the angel of the Lord would pass through Egypt, striking down the firstborn sons of the Egyptians but "passing over" any house marked with the lamb's blood. Meanwhile, the Israelites were to roast the lamb and eat it with bitter herbs and unleavened bread, ready to depart Egypt in haste (Exodus 12:8–11).

This event is both a historical deliverance and a perpetual memorial. The immediate purpose of the Passover sacrifice was to protect the Israelites from the destructive final plague. The blood on the doorpost signified obedience and faith in God's word, setting them apart from judgment. In a larger theological sense, Passover became an annual commemoration of God's saving power and covenant faithfulness. Exodus 12:14 declares, "This is a day you are to commemorate; for the generations to come you shall celebrate it as a festival to the Lord—a lasting ordinance".

The significance of the Passover lamb's sacrifice resonates far beyond the single night of Israel's exodus. Historically, it inaugurated the great event of liberation from slavery. Liturgically, it established a pattern of remembrance, reinforcing that God had acted decisively to redeem His people. Symbolically, the themes of redemption, the lamb's substitutionary role, and the importance of sacrificial blood continued to shape Israel's identity. In later biblical revelation, the New Testament identifies Jesus with the Passover lamb (1 Corinthians 5:7), seeing in His crucifixion the ultimate form of protection and deliverance from the bondage of sin.

For those living at the time of the exodus, the sacrifice underscored the immediate urgency of trusting God's commands. Unlike previous plagues, where the Israelites were often spared automatically, in this final plague they had a part to play: they had to act in faith by slaughtering the lamb and applying its blood. This obedience exemplifies the essence of sacrificial faith—living in accordance with divine instruction to receive divine deliverance.

Passover stands out, then, as both an historical pivot (ushering

Israel out of Egypt) and a spiritual blueprint for understanding how God saves and claims His people. While subsequent generations in Israel would refine and renew the Passover regulations (Deuteronomy 16:1–8), this inaugural event laid the template for a redemption that resonated through the centuries, culminating ultimately in the New Testament teachings that the blood of the true Lamb, Christ, "speaks a better word" (Hebrews 12:24).

Conclusion

In summary, the earliest sacrificial practices in Scripture serve as foundational signposts. They point forward to the greater redemptive acts of God while revealing fundamental truths about worship, sin, grace, and faith. They show both the depth of human need and the breadth of divine compassion. As we progress into the rich tapestry of sacrifices in later biblical texts (a discussion outside the scope of this chapter), we carry these lessons with us: that genuine sacrifice, whether personal or communal, arises from heartfelt devotion, occurs in the context of God's revealed will, and points ultimately to a reconciliation between sinful humanity and the God who desires to dwell among His people.

CHAPTER 2: THE BURNT OFFERING (OLAH)

Among the various sacrifices detailed in the Old Testament, the *burnt offering* (Hebrew: עוֹלָה, *Olah*) stands out for its unique requirement that the entire sacrificial animal be consumed on the altar. This characteristic reflects a total dedication to God, symbolizing the worshipper's complete surrender. In the Book of Leviticus, the burnt offering is the first type of sacrifice described in depth (Leviticus 1:1–17), indicating its foundational role in Israelite worship.

The prominence of the burnt offering can be traced throughout much of the Torah. By studying its specific regulations, one gains insight not only into the outward ritual but also into the heart posture that God desires from His people. The requirement that it be wholly consumed—leaving no part to be eaten by the worshipper—communicates a profound message of consecration, reminding us that true worship touches every aspect of one's life. In addition, the burnt offering sets a precedent for the concept of a "pleasing aroma" ascending before the Lord, a motif repeated whenever sacrifices are wholeheartedly offered in faith and obedience (Genesis 8:20–21; Leviticus 1:9).

Section 1: Old Testament Background of the Burnt Offering

1.1 Etymology and Core Meaning

The Hebrew word עוֹלָה (*Olah*) is derived from a root meaning "to ascend," reflecting the idea that the smoke of the offering rises upward to God. This symbolic image underlies the entire practice: as the animal is completely burned on the altar, its essence (represented by the rising smoke) ascends to the heavens, signifying total dedication and the worshipper's desire to draw near to God. This same root appears in words related to going up or ascending, emphasizing that the burnt offering is, by nature, directed entirely toward the Lord.

1.2 Distinction from Other Types of Sacrifices

While later chapters of this book examine other sacrificial categories—such as the sin offering (*Chatat*), the guilt offering (*Asham*), and the peace offering (*Shelamim*)—the burnt offering stands apart in its procedures and symbolism. In a sin offering, for instance, only specific parts of the animal might be burned, with the priest or worshipper sometimes consuming certain portions. In a burnt offering, however, the whole animal (with only minor exceptions like the hide in certain contexts) is offered up. This total consumption underscores the principle of unreserved dedication. Rather than allowing the worshipper or the priests to partake of any part of the sacrifice, the entire gift is relinquished to God alone.

This characteristic highlights a core purpose of the burnt offering: **it symbolizes a complete surrender of the worshipper's life and resources to God.** Consequently, one might view the burnt offering as a fundamental expression of homage and reverence, preparing the way for deeper fellowship offerings or specific atonement sacrifices. Although *olah* sacrifices were often made in tandem with other rituals, Leviticus begins with their regulations to establish the foundational concept that *God deserves our all.*

Section 2: Procedure of the Burnt Offering

2.1 Selection of the Animal

The instructions in Leviticus 1:2 specify that the burnt offering could come from the herd (cattle) or the flock (sheep or goats). Leviticus 1:14 additionally includes provisions for offering birds (turtledoves or pigeons) if the worshipper could not afford larger livestock, ensuring that all Israelites could participate regardless of economic status. Across each category, the animal was to be "without defect" (Leviticus 1:3), reflecting the standard that offerings to God must be the very best, symbolizing moral and spiritual purity.

This requirement of a "blameless" or "unblemished" animal foreshadows the later biblical theme that only a pure and spotless substitute is acceptable in God's sight. Moreover, the principle that worshippers should bring the best they can afford—from the most luxurious option for wealthier individuals to the simpler but still valid bird offering for the poor—reinforces the inclusive nature of Israel's sacrificial system.

2.2 Presentation before the Lord

After selecting the appropriate animal, the worshipper was instructed to bring it "to the entrance to the tent of meeting" (Leviticus 1:3). This public act acknowledged that sacrifice is not merely a private transaction but a communal and covenantal event. By bringing the offering to the designated place of worship, the individual demonstrated a readiness to align with the corporate life of Israel under God's covenant.

In later eras, once the Temple was built in Jerusalem, the burnt offerings were presented in the Temple precincts. However, the principle remained the same: worshippers approached God in the manner and location prescribed by Him, underscoring His holiness and sovereignty.

2.3 The Laying On of Hands

Leviticus 1:4 states that the individual offering the sacrifice "is to lay his hand on the head of the burnt offering, and it will be accepted on his behalf to make atonement for him". This action—often referred to as *semikah* in Hebrew tradition—carries profound symbolism. By placing his hand on the animal's head, the worshipper identifies himself with the sacrifice, acknowledging that this creature stands in his place. Although the burnt offering was not strictly a sin offering, the concept of atonement is still present, implying a transfer of sorts: the worshipper's devotion and need for acceptance before God are embodied in the gift placed on the altar.

Some interpreters also see this gesture as the worshipper's pledge of total allegiance and recognition that, apart from divine grace, no one can stand justified before a holy God. The sacrificial animal thus becomes a means of approach, enabling the worshipper to draw near to God in faith.

2.4 Slaughter and Blood Manipulation

In the burnt offering ritual, the worshipper (not the priest) typically carried out the slaughter of the animal (Leviticus 1:5). This detail underscores the personal involvement expected of each Israelite; sacrifice was never intended to be a distant or purely ritualistic act. The worshipper's role in the animal's death underscores the gravity of approaching God, reminding him that the gift of life is being offered.

After the animal was slain, the priest collected the blood and sprinkled it around the altar. Blood, in biblical thought, represented life (Leviticus 17:11). The sprinkling of the blood on the sides of the altar signified the consecration of both the gift and the place of worship. It also underscored that atonement—*kippur*—requires the life-force that resides in the blood. While the burnt offering may often be seen as a sign of worshipful devotion, Leviticus remains clear that blood is indispensable for reconciliation with God.

2.5 Preparation for Burning

Following the sprinkling of the blood, the animal's carcass was skinned (by the worshipper or, in some instructions, by the priests), and then the meat was cut into pieces as specified in Leviticus 1:6–9. Particular attention was given to washing the internal organs and legs, symbolizing ritual purity. This careful process conveyed the seriousness and respect owed to God's sanctuary.

The priests then arranged the wood on the altar and laid the pieces of the animal in order, making certain that the entire offering would be consumed by fire. In the case of a bird offering (Leviticus 1:14–17), the process was adapted accordingly, but the principle remained: the offering was fully given over to the flames.

2.6 Total Consumption by Fire

The defining feature of the burnt offering is that it was completely burned—reduced to ashes on the altar. Unlike other sacrifices in which the priests or worshippers might eat part of the meat, this entire offering ascended to God in the form of smoke. Leviticus repeatedly mentions that this was "an offering made by fire, an aroma pleasing to the Lord" (Leviticus 1:9, 1:17; 2:9).

The phrase "pleasing aroma" conveys the acceptance of the offering by God. In ancient Near Eastern contexts, the notion of a deity "smelling" an offering symbolized divine favor and acknowledgement. For the Israelites, this imagery served to remind them that their devotion, when brought with sincerity and obedience, was pleasing to the Lord of heaven and earth.

2.7 Perpetual Burnt Offering

While Leviticus 1 describes the general procedure for individuals, other passages (Exodus 29:38–42; Numbers 28:1–8) outline the daily burnt offerings that the priesthood was required to perform on behalf of the entire community—one lamb in the morning and another at twilight. This perpetual burnt offering ensured a constant expression of Israel's dedication to God, day by day, sunrise to sunset.

Moreover, Leviticus 6:8–13 details instructions for keeping the altar's fire continually burning. The priests were to remove the ashes regularly and add fresh wood so that the fire never went out (Leviticus 6:12–13). Symbolically, this perpetual fire reflected the unceasing nature of worship and the enduring presence of God among His people.

Section 3: Purpose of the Burnt Offering

3.1 Expression of Total Devotion

Foremost among the reasons for offering a burnt sacrifice was to declare complete commitment to the Lord. Because the *olah* was entirely consumed, it stood as a powerful gesture of surrender, acknowledging God's sovereignty and worthiness to receive the worshipper's whole being. In many cases, individuals voluntarily brought this offering as an act of adoration or thanksgiving. As Psalm 51:16–17 reminds us, God desires a contrite heart over mere ritual, yet the ritual of the burnt offering provided a tangible avenue for expressing humility and reverence.

3.2 Atonement and Reconciliation

Although the sin offering (*Chatat*) is more commonly associated with forgiveness of sins, the burnt offering also carried atoning significance. Leviticus 1:4 explicitly states that the burnt offering "will be accepted on his behalf to make atonement for him". The worshipper's identification with the sacrifice, the shedding and sprinkling of blood, and the complete burning of the animal combined to create a ritual that facilitated renewed fellowship with God.

Some interpreters note that the Hebrew concept of atonement (*kippur*) can encompass both covering sin and purifying from defilement. In the burnt offering, the focus is often on restoring a right relationship through an act of wholehearted devotion. Although the primary emphasis of *olah* might be worship, this dimension of reconciliation should not be overlooked.

3.3 Thanksgiving and Celebration

Beyond atonement, burnt offerings could also serve as expressions of gratitude for divine blessings or deliverances. For example, after significant military victories or times of national thanksgiving, Israelites might bring burnt offerings in recognition of God's help. The communal burnt offerings offered during festivals (such as the Feast of Tabernacles or the Feast of Unleavened Bread) further highlight the burnt offering's function in collective worship.

In these situations, the *olah* was not limited to a remedy for sin but also served to unite the people in acknowledging God's provision. The act of consecrating an entire animal underscored the worshipper's conviction that all blessings ultimately belonged to the Lord, and only by His grace did Israel enjoy peace and prosperity.

3.4 Consecration of Priests and Objects

Leviticus 8 describes the consecration of Aaron and his sons for the priesthood. As part of that ceremony, Moses offered a burnt offering to the Lord (Leviticus 8:18–21). This underscores the role of the *olah* in setting aside people or objects for holy service. The total consumption of the animal paralleled the complete dedication expected of those who ministered before God. Similarly, in various stages of the tabernacle's inauguration, burnt offerings were central to sanctifying the space where God's presence would dwell (Exodus 29:10–46).

Section 4: Significance for Israel's Worship and Beyond

4.1 Reflecting Israel's Identity as a Holy Nation

Israel's sacrificial system, and especially the burnt offering, was integral to the nation's identity as "a kingdom of priests and a holy nation" (Exodus 19:6). The burnt offering, often performed daily at the tabernacle (and later, the Temple), served as a visible sign of Israel's ongoing devotion to Yahweh. As the smoke rose from the altar each morning and evening, the people were reminded of their covenant bond, their obligations of faithfulness, and God's gracious willingness to dwell among them.

This recurrent image of fire and smoke, sustained day and night, symbolized not only the unceasing worship of God but also His continuing acceptance of and care for His people. Even when individuals were unaware or going about their daily tasks, the altar's perpetual flame underscored the living reality of God's holiness in their midst.

4.2 Moral and Spiritual Lessons

The thoroughly consumed nature of the burnt offering illustrated key moral and spiritual lessons. First, the worshipper's participation—from selecting an unblemished animal to placing their hand upon its head—fostered personal responsibility. Faith in the God of Israel was to be neither theoretical nor detached; it involved direct engagement. Second, the ritual made clear that approaching God came at a cost. Though forgiveness and relationship are offered by grace, atonement demands recognition that life is precious and that devotion cannot be half-hearted.

Furthermore, the requirement that the animal be the best the worshipper could offer pointed the Israelite's gaze to a future hope: a time when God Himself would provide the perfect sacrifice, directing to the consummation of sacrifice in the Messiah (a subject addressed more fully in the later chapters of this book).

4.3 Corporate and Individual Dimensions

Because the Torah called for both communal and individual burnt offerings, the *olah* was more than a private act of piety. Nationally, Israel presented daily burnt offerings on the people's behalf, reinforcing the collective responsibility to uphold the covenant. On an individual level, a worshipper could bring a burnt offering for personal devotion or special occasions of thanksgiving.

This dual aspect underscores the robust understanding of community within Israel's worship. The entire nation was bound together under the same covenant obligations, yet each person retained the privilege and duty to draw near to God personally. Through the *olah*, worshippers expressed both their unity as God's people and their personal dedication to Him, bridging the communal and the intimate.

Conclusion

In summary, the burnt offering taught Israel—and continues to teach modern believers—that worship is all-encompassing. The flames that consumed the sacrifice also consumed the worshipper's illusions of casual, halfhearted piety. Standing before God with an unblemished offering, the worshipper confessed both dependence and dedication. In return, God promised acceptance and fellowship, indicated by the "pleasing aroma." This divine-human exchange, simple yet profound, remains a key to understanding the depth and beauty of biblical sacrifice, underscoring that the life of faith is a continual journey of surrender, communion, and renewal in the presence of the living God.

CHAPTER 3: THE GRAIN OFFERING (MINCHAH)

In the Israelite sacrificial system, offerings took multiple forms to express varying facets of worship, dependence, and covenant life. Among these, the *Grain Offering*—referred to in Hebrew as the מִנְחָה (*Minchah*)—occupied a unique place. Unlike animal sacrifices, which involved the shedding of blood, the Grain Offering focused on the produce of the land, particularly flour mixed with oil and frankincense.

While the Burnt Offering (*Olah*) symbolized complete dedication through consuming the entire animal on the altar, and the Sin Offering (*Chatat*) emphasized atonement for wrongdoing, the Grain Offering had a distinct purpose: it was a gift of homage, thanksgiving, and fellowship, reflecting the worshipper's daily sustenance and labor. From the perspective of ancient Israel, *Minchah* conveyed a sense of gratitude for God's provision and blessing on the fields, with the act of offering bread-like substances on the altar highlighting Israel's reliance on the God who gives life and sustains His people.

Section 1: Biblical Basis for the Grain Offering

1.1 Scriptural Foundations in Leviticus

The most comprehensive treatment of the Grain Offering appears in the Book of Leviticus, specifically **Leviticus 2:1–16** and **Leviticus 6:14–23**. These passages provide the foundation for understanding the diverse ways a *Minchah* could be prepared and presented. From these texts, we learn that individuals were permitted some flexibility in how they brought the offering—whether as fine flour alone, or baked, fried, or cooked in a pan (Leviticus 2:4–10). This adaptability allowed different socio-economic groups and households to participate, whether they had access to baking ovens or simpler cooking utensils.

Leviticus 2 begins by stating, "When anyone brings a *grain offering* to the Lord, their offering is to be of the finest flour" (Leviticus 2:1). The Hebrew word translated as "finest flour" conveys that the best product from the harvested grain was to be reserved for God's service. This emphasis on quality reflects a broader biblical principle: that God deserves the best of what we have, as an acknowledgment that everything ultimately comes from Him (Proverbs 3:9).

1.2 The Broader Use of 'Minchah'

Outside of Leviticus, the term *minchah* can simply mean "gift" or "tribute." For instance, in Genesis 32:13–21, Jacob sends a "gift" (*minchah*) to his brother Esau in hopes of appeasing him. Similarly, 1 Samuel 10:27 mentions certain individuals refusing to bring *minchah* (tribute) to King Saul. Thus, the concept of *minchah* in the Bible is not always tied to sacrificial ritual; it can refer generally to an offering of goods or produce given in respect or as an act of homage.

When the Torah applies the word *minchah* to the context of sacrifices, it captures the notion that the offering is a **tribute** to God—the ultimate King—recognizing His lordship over the land and everything it yields. This theological dimension remains central to the Grain Offering: it is the worshipper's tangible acknowledgment that God is the divine provider, worthy of homage.

Section 2: Procedure for Presenting the Grain Offering

2.1 The Handful for Burning

According to Leviticus 2:2, when a worshipper brought the Grain Offering to the priests, the officiating priest would take a "memorial portion," a handful of the flour (or portion of the baked item) along with oil and all the frankincense, and burn it on the altar. This act served as "an offering made by fire, an aroma pleasing to the Lord" (Leviticus 2:2).

The idea of a "memorial portion" (Hebrew: אַזְכָּרָה, *azkarah*) signifies that a part of the offering was devoted entirely to God, going up in smoke as a gesture of praise and remembrance. The aroma was understood to be *pleasing* to God, echoing a recurring motif in sacrificial literature (cf. Genesis 8:21). In offering even a small portion to be fully consumed, the worshipper expressed that the entire produce, in fact, belongs to God.

2.2 The Remainder for the Priests

After the priest removed and burned the handful, the remainder belonged to Aaron's sons, the priestly family. This grain portion served as part of their sustenance, underscoring the principle that those who minister in the sanctuary derive their livelihood from the offerings presented by the community (1 Corinthians 9:13). In this way, the Grain Offering not only honored God but also provided for the priests, reinforcing the sense of community interdependence embedded within the sacrificial system.

2.3 Baked, Fried, or Uncooked

Leviticus 2:4–10 delineates different forms the Grain Offering could take. It could be:

- **Uncooked Fine Flour**: Mixed with oil and frankincense.
- **Baked in the Oven**: Typically unleavened cakes or wafers spread with oil.
- **Cooked on a Griddle**: Unleavened dough mixed with oil and then broken into pieces.
- **Prepared in a Pan**: A form of baked dough with oil, perhaps something akin to a thick cake.

In each case, the central components—flour and oil—remained the same, and frankincense was often added for its fragrant quality. These variations allowed worshippers to bring a Grain Offering that reflected their household's capacity and method of preparation. Yet the underlying principle remained uniform: no matter the cooking style, part of the offering was burned on the altar, while the rest was allocated to the priests.

2.4 No Yeast or Honey, But Salt

A distinctive requirement for the Grain Offering was the prohibition of yeast (*chametz*) or honey, along with the mandatory inclusion of salt (Leviticus 2:11–13). Yeast and honey were not intrinsically sinful elements; in fact, the Israelites regularly consumed bread with yeast and used honey as a sweetener. However, within the context of the sanctuary, yeast symbolized fermentation or corruption, and honey—due to its rapid fermentation under heat—may have been similarly perceived.

Salt, on the other hand, was required in "all your grain offerings" (Leviticus 2:13). Salt, known for its preservative and purifying qualities, became a symbol of covenant faithfulness and longevity (Numbers 18:19, referred to as a "covenant of salt"). Including salt in the Grain Offering thus represented an enduring, incorruptible commitment between the worshipper and God.

Section 3: Ingredients and Their Symbolism

3.1 Fine Flour

The requirement of fine flour indicated that the worshipper brought the very best of their agricultural product to God. This detail parallels the standard of offering an animal "without defect" in blood sacrifices. By ensuring the flour was meticulously ground and refined, the worshipper demonstrated care, reverence, and the priority of giving God what was excellent. Fine flour might also point to the labor and diligence behind the offering: it was the product of winnowing, grinding, and sifting—processes that required effort and time.

From a theological standpoint, fine flour underscores the truth that genuine worship involves both **quality** and **intentionality**. Just as a worshipper would not bring a diseased or second-rate animal for a burnt offering, so too they were to avoid offering coarse or subpar grain for the *Minchah*. By presenting the fruit of diligent labor, the worshipper declared that honoring God was worth their best effort.

3.2 Oil

Oil served multiple functions in ancient Israel—lighting lamps, anointing kings or priests, and, of course, cooking and baking. In the Grain Offering, mixing or spreading oil with the flour not only bound the ingredients together but also introduced the connotation of **spiritual and ceremonial anointing**. Throughout Scripture, oil often symbolizes the Holy Spirit's presence or divine blessing (cf. 1 Samuel 16:13, Isaiah 61:1).

While Leviticus does not explicitly interpret oil in that manner, later Jewish and Christian traditions have frequently drawn the parallel between oil and the presence or favor of God. Thus, offering flour and oil could be seen as presenting one's daily resources infused with God's sanctifying presence.

3.3 Frankincense

Frankincense, a costly and fragrant resin, was also part of the Grain Offering, at least in its uncooked form (Leviticus 2:1–2). When burned on the altar, frankincense released a sweet-smelling smoke, contributing to the "pleasing aroma" before the Lord. This ingredient enhanced the sense of beauty, awe, and respect within the sacrificial act.

Moreover, frankincense was commonly used in worship throughout the ancient Near East, signifying reverence for a deity. In the Israelite context, adding frankincense likely highlighted the distinct holiness of God and the sacredness of the offering. The rising fragrance visually and symbolically represented the ascent of the worshipper's praise and devotion.

3.4 Salt: Covenant and Purity

As mentioned, salt was indispensable in all Grain Offerings (Leviticus 2:13). Salt's preservative nature prevented decay and spoilage, linking it to the idea of permanence. The phrase "covenant of salt" (Numbers 18:19; 2 Chronicles 13:5) indicates an unbreakable alliance, emphasizing durability and fidelity.

In the daily realm, salt also enhances flavor, suggesting that offerings to God should be both pure and "pleasing" in the sense of being carefully seasoned. Including salt declared that the worshipper's intentions were loyal and enduring: just as salt keeps food from corruption, so the worshipper sought a lasting covenant relationship with the Lord, free from the corruption of insincerity or halfheartedness.

Section 4: Purpose of the Grain Offering

4.1 Thanksgiving and Acknowledgment of Divine Provision

One of the clearest purposes of the Grain Offering was to express **gratitude** for God's sustenance. In an agrarian society, harvests were paramount for survival. By offering the first and best of their produce to God, Israelites affirmed that their fields, flocks, and families were sustained by the Almighty's hand. Leviticus 23:9–14 later instituted the *Feast of Firstfruits*, which shared a similar principle of dedicating the initial yield of the land to God.

Moreover, the Grain Offering could be brought independently or alongside other offerings (e.g., the Burnt Offering or Peace Offering) to underscore the worshipper's posture of thanksgiving. The quiet, bloodless nature of the *Minchah* contrasted with the more dramatic scenes of animal sacrifice, highlighting the everyday nature of worship and the reality that praising God need not always involve shedding blood.

4.2 Sanctification of Daily Labor

The biblical faith consistently weaves together the "sacred" and the "mundane." Unlike religious systems that sharply divide worship from ordinary life, Israel's sacrificial system encouraged the sanctification of everyday existence. The Grain Offering exemplifies this principle: bread, a basic staple, became an offering worthy of the altar.

This sanctification of daily labor teaches the valuable lesson that God's presence extends beyond moments of formal worship. Tilling the soil, grinding grain, and preparing bread are all part of a holistic devotion to God. The worshipper's daily efforts can be seen as acts of service to the Creator, who grants the earth's fertility.

4.3 Communal Support

Because the leftover grain (after a handful was burned) was given to the priests, the Grain Offering also served a practical community function. Priests, whose primary role was leading worship and performing sacred duties, relied on the offerings for sustenance. Their focus on ministerial responsibilities was sustained by the contributions of the community.

By sharing their produce, ordinary Israelites played a part in maintaining the worship center and enabling the priests to fulfill their calling. This dynamic solidified community bonds and reminded everyone that worship was not a solitary endeavor. Rather, it was a collective experience, tying people together under God's provision and care.

4.4 Voluntary Expression of Devotion

In many instances, the Grain Offering was voluntarily offered as a gesture of personal devotion. Although certain mandatory offerings involved grain (especially in conjunction with other rituals), individuals could also choose to bring a *Minchah* as a freewill expression of praise or petition. Such spontaneity fostered a vibrant worship life, where people were not restricted to set times or events but could seek and honor God in moments of personal conviction or thanksgiving.

This freedom to bring a Grain Offering at one's own initiative demonstrates that worship in Israelite practice combined both structured rites and personal piety. The structure taught theological truths and ensured consistency, while voluntary acts allowed for heartfelt, situational devotion, reflecting the dynamic relationship between God and His covenant people.

Section 5: Theological Significance

5.1 Holistic Worship: Body and Soul

While most sacrifices in Israel involved blood and thus spoke loudly of atonement, the Grain Offering focused on **worship** more broadly. Animal sacrifices often addressed sin or covenant violations, but the Grain Offering centered on daily dependence and honor. This distinction shows that a believer's relationship with God encompasses more than forgiveness alone; it includes **recognition, homage, and gratitude** for all aspects of life.

Through the *Minchah*, the worshipper brought the fruit of their labor—symbolic of physical, bodily work—and consecrated it to the Lord. In this way, worship was not confined to matters of guilt and atonement but extended to the entire spectrum of human activity. Spiritual fellowship with God involved the realm of bread-making and field-tending just as much as the solemnities of sin removal.

5.2 Anticipation of Spiritual Sustenance

Christian interpreters have often identified foreshadowings of Christ throughout the Old Testament sacrificial system. The burnt offering, sin offering, and guilt offering each illuminate different dimensions of Jesus' work on the cross. The Grain Offering, though less explicit, has also been seen as a type that hints toward Christ as the **Bread of Life** (John 6:35).

In this perspective, the use of bread and oil in the *Minchah* prefigures the spiritual nourishment Jesus provides. Just as ancient Israelites recognized God as the ultimate provider of grain, Christians see Jesus as the source of spiritual sustenance.

5.3 Worship from the Ordinary

A critical message of the Grain Offering is that **the ordinary can be made holy** when offered to God. Flour, oil, and frankincense were commonplace items in the ancient Near

Eastern household (though frankincense was more precious). There was nothing inherently exalted about flour or dough—yet in placing them on the altar with sincerity, they became an act of sacred worship.

This truth resonates powerfully in any era: human labor and daily resources can become instruments of praise. Whether one is a farmer, a baker, or engaged in modern professions, the Grain Offering provides a blueprint for integrating faith with vocation. In acknowledging that one's livelihood is a divine gift, it becomes natural to dedicate the fruit of that labor back to the Giver.

5.4 Remembrance and Relationship

The small portion burned on the altar was often called a "memorial portion" (Leviticus 2:2, 2:9). While the word can suggest a "reminder" to God of the worshipper's devotion, it also indicates that the offering stands as a tangible sign of the covenant relationship. The Grain Offering united the physical and spiritual dimensions, reminding worshippers that every harvest, every loaf, every meal, is an occasion to remember God's kindness.

Section 6: Practical Reflections and Contemporary Relevance

6.1 Lessons for Devotional Life

For those seeking to apply these ancient practices to modern faith contexts, the Grain Offering highlights the importance of **thanksgiving** and **dependence** on God. Believers today, who often no longer live in agrarian settings, can still glean from the principle that the fruit of our labor—our finances, our creative work, our time—should be offered back to God in acknowledgment of His provision.

Regular giving, tithes, and offerings within a church or charitable context can be viewed through the lens of *Minchah*: not merely a financial transaction, but a sanctifying moment in which one's work is consecrated to God. Similarly, acts of service or hospitality can be perceived as bread-like offerings, symbolic of our daily routines being placed on the "altar" of worship.

6.2 The Role of Cheerful Giving

While Leviticus' instructions are often detailed and procedural, the underlying spirit of the Grain Offering embraces **cheerful giving**. The worshipper brought fine flour, possibly the best portion of their field's yield, voluntarily and joyfully. This resonates with Paul's teaching that "God loves a cheerful giver" (2 Corinthians 9:7,). The synergy between Old and New Testament understanding of worship highlights a consistent message: giving to God should be marked by gratitude, not begrudging obligation.

6.3 Elevating the Mundane

In a world that sometimes compartmentalizes the "sacred" and the "secular," the *Minchah* reminds us that even the most ordinary products of labor—grain and oil—can be offered as an act of spiritual devotion. The line between sacred and secular is thus blurred, if not erased, when we live under the conviction that all we have is from the Lord. Whether one bakes bread for communion, volunteers time at a food bank, or supports a household through a standard job, the principle remains: we can lift up our work as an offering of thanks and honor to God.

Conclusion

Symbolically, the Grain Offering reveals key dimensions of Israel's religious life. It tangibly connected worship with labor, reminding the community that all blessings stem from God's goodness. It also underscored the principle of giving one's best as a tribute, acknowledging the Lord's sovereign rule. The presence of salt, the absence of yeast or honey, and the addition of frankincense show that precise instructions guided the offering's purity and significance, yet the final objective was consistently relational: to express devotion and trust toward God who sustains His people.

Even after the formal sacrificial system ceased with the destruction of the Temple, the theological truths behind the Grain Offering remain instructive. Modern believers can reflect on the *Minchah* to cultivate a daily posture of thankful worship, seeing their work and resources as gifts to be shared. In the broad narrative of Scripture, the Grain Offering contributes a distinct note in the symphony of sacrifice—an offering that points beyond itself to a God who delights in heartfelt gratitude, who provides for every need, and who desires that all aspects of life be given over in joyful worship.

CHAPTER 4: THE PEACE OFFERING (SHELAMIM)

The Peace Offering, known in Hebrew as שְׁלָמִים (*Shelamim*), occupies a distinctive position within the Old Testament sacrificial system. While other offerings often center on atonement, guilt, or total surrender, the Peace Offering emphasizes **fellowship and shared communion** between the worshipper, the priests, and God. Frequently translated as "Peace Offering," "Fellowship Offering," or "Well-Being Offering," the term *Shelamim* derives from the root word related to **shalom**, connoting wholeness, well-being, and harmony. Thus, the Peace Offering underscores the communal and celebratory dimensions of worship in ancient Israel.

Section 1: Biblical Basis and Terminology

1.1 Scriptural Foundations

The primary instructions for the Peace Offering appear in

Leviticus 3 and **Leviticus 7:11–36**. These passages detail how the animal must be without defect and how the offerer, the priests, and the altar each play a specific role in the sacrifice. Notably, Leviticus 3 uses the phrase "if someone's offering is a fellowship offering" (Leviticus 3:1), underscoring that this sacrifice was distinct from the Burnt Offering, Sin Offering, or Guilt Offering. The Peace Offering could come from the herd (cattle), the flock (sheep or goats), and had to be free from blemish or deformity (Leviticus 3:6–7).

Further clarification in Leviticus 7 establishes that the Peace Offering can be given for different reasons, such as **thanksgiving**, **fulfilling a vow**, or **voluntary devotion** (Leviticus 7:11–16). Each motive slightly influenced how the sacrifice was prepared and how quickly the meat had to be consumed. Nevertheless, the consistent theme is that this offering was intended to celebrate and acknowledge harmonious relationship—with God, among the worshippers, and within the covenant community.

1.2 The Meaning of "Shelamim"

The Hebrew term *Shelamim* arises from the same root as **shalom**, commonly translated "peace." Yet *shalom* encompasses far more than the absence of conflict; it signifies well-being, prosperity, wholeness, and right relationship. Hence, a *Shelamim* offering could be understood as a "wholeness" or "completeness" offering. When Israelites brought a Peace Offering, they were effectively entering a symbolic state of well-being and solidarity with God.

In many biblical narratives, peace offerings appear in contexts of celebration or reconciliation. For example, after the people of Israel collectively repented or experienced deliverance, they often offered peace offerings as part of worship (Judges 20:26, where the Israelites offered burnt offerings and fellowship offerings after a communal crisis). The name itself highlights that this sacrifice was bound up with fellowship, gratitude, and covenant renewal.

Section 2: Different Types of Peace Offerings

2.1 Thanksgiving Offering (Todah)

The Peace Offering included a special category sometimes called the **"Thanksgiving Offering"** (Hebrew: תּוֹדָה, *Todah*). Leviticus 7:12–15 describes how if the Peace Offering was brought as a thanksgiving offering, it had to be accompanied by **cakes of bread** made without yeast, mixed with oil, and also loaves of bread with yeast. A portion of these breads went to the priest, and the rest was to be eaten by the worshipper on the same day.

This requirement to **consume the meat and breads on the same day** (Leviticus 7:15) emphasized the immediacy and intensity of gratitude: the worshipper's thanks to God was to be expressed wholeheartedly and without delay. The Thanksgiving Offering typically recognized divine blessing, healing, or deliverance—situations in which the worshipper felt moved to praise God tangibly.

2.2 Vow Offering (Neder)

When a person made a vow to the Lord, they might fulfill it by presenting a Peace Offering called a **Vow Offering** (Leviticus 7:16). The vow could concern a variety of commitments: for instance, pledging to donate resources to the sanctuary or to dedicate a period of special devotion to God.

Once the vow was complete, the worshipper sealed that commitment with a Peace Offering, demonstrating thankfulness for God's help in fulfilling the vow.

In this scenario, the worshipper could consume the meat over two days rather than one (Leviticus 7:16–17), reflecting a slightly extended celebration of God's faithfulness. At the same time, the sacrifice underscored the worshipper's sense of integrity—**the vow was kept**, and the offering served as both closure and public witness to that fact.

2.3 Freewill Offering (Nedavah)

A third category under the umbrella of the Peace Offering is the **Freewill Offering**. This was wholly voluntary, not tied to a vow or a specific occasion of thanksgiving. Rather, it expressed a **spontaneous act of devotion** or worship. Leviticus 7:16–18 indicates that the regulations for consuming the meat were akin to those for the Vow Offering, allowing for consumption on the day of sacrifice and the following day.

The Freewill Offering highlights the openhearted nature of worship in Israel's sacrificial system: people could approach God **out of sheer gratitude or devotion** at any time, without needing a crisis or a specific event as impetus. This readiness to give spontaneously further illustrates the communal and joyful atmosphere inherent in the Peace Offering.

Section 3: Procedure and Distribution of the Peace Offering

3.1 Laying On of Hands and Slaughter

Like other animal sacrifices, the Peace Offering required the worshipper to lay hands on the head of the chosen animal at the entrance of the tent of meeting (Leviticus 3:2). This symbolic gesture indicated identification: the worshipper's personal investment in the offering, a confession that life was being offered on their behalf to honor or commune with God. The person then slaughtered the animal, while the priests collected its blood.

Although the Peace Offering is not primarily about atoning for sin, **blood remained significant** for ritual purity and covenant consecration. As Leviticus 17:11 reminds us, "the life of a creature is in the blood," and thus blood was central to any sacrifice that established or reflected relationship with God. The priests sprinkled the blood on the sides of the altar, visually demonstrating that this was a sacred, life-giving act.

3.2 Burning the Fat Portions

One distinctive aspect of the Peace Offering procedure was how specific **fatty portions** of the animal—covering the internal organs—were burned on the altar. Leviticus 3:3–5 details that all the fat around the kidneys, intestines, and the covering over the liver was to be removed and offered on the altar as an "aroma pleasing to the Lord." This signified giving the **richest and choicest** parts directly to God.

The prohibition against eating certain fats and blood (Leviticus 7:23–27) highlights the sanctity of life and the principle that the best belongs to the Lord. In ancient Near Eastern culture, fat was considered a prized portion—often associated with abundance—so dedicating it to God underscored reverence and honor.

3.3 Portions for the Priests

Unlike the Burnt Offering, which was wholly consumed on the altar, or the Grain Offering, whose major portion went to the priests, the Peace Offering was divided among God, the priests, and the worshipper. According to Leviticus 7:28–34, the officiating priest received the **breast** (the wave offering) and the **right thigh** (the heave offering) as their share. Waving or heaving these portions before the Lord symbolized dedicating them to God before granting them to the priest.

This division reflected the **corporate aspect** of the sacrifice: it was an occasion in which the priesthood also participated in the meal, reminding Israel that the priestly class served as mediators and ministers on their behalf. Receiving these portions allowed the priests to share in the people's joy and gratitude while providing sustenance for their families.

3.4 Communal Meal for the Worshipper and Family

The most remarkable feature of the Peace Offering was that **the worshipper and their household or guests ate the remaining meat** of the sacrifice. Leviticus 7:15–18 provides the guidelines for how quickly the meat had to be consumed, depending on the type of Peace Offering (Thanksgiving vs. Vow/Freewill).

In the Thanksgiving Offering, consumption had to occur on the same day, fostering an atmosphere of **immediate celebration** and festivity. For Vow or Freewill Offerings, the meat could be eaten on the day of sacrifice or the next day, but any leftover by the third day had to be burned. This regulated time frame ensured the meal remained a sacred act, guarded against corruption or spoilage. It also heightened the sense of rejoicing in God's presence, as friends and family gathered to share the meal in or near the sanctuary courts.

Section 4: Purpose and Significance of the Peace Offering

4.1 Celebration of Divine Goodness

The Peace Offering served as a tangible means of **celebrating God's goodness**—especially in contexts of thanksgiving, fulfilled vows, or spontaneous devotion. When an Israelite encountered a special blessing (harvest success, safe travel, personal deliverance from calamity), it was fitting to come before the Lord with a *Shelamim* offering, publicly acknowledging that "the Lord has dealt bountifully with me" (Psalm 13:6).

In an agricultural society, victory over famine, pests, or enemies warranted communal rejoicing. The Peace Offering institutionalized a practice of turning blessings into worship, preventing complacency or forgetfulness. Rather than attributing success to personal merit alone, the worshipper recognized God as the source of every good gift (Deuteronomy 8:17–18).

4.2 Reinforcing Covenant Fellowship

Another vital dimension of the Peace Offering was **covenantal fellowship**. By participating in a shared meal—God (symbolically receiving the burnt fat portions), the priest, and the worshipper (and household)—the entire community reaffirmed unity under the covenant. Leviticus 7:15–16 suggests a joyful communion made possible by being in right standing with God.

Symbolically, one might say God hosted the meal: the altar served as His table, and the worshipper and priest received invitations to dine. This portrayal of divine-human fellowship resonates throughout Scripture. In Exodus 24:9–11, for instance, the elders of Israel ate and drank in God's presence at Mount Sinai. The Peace Offering carried that same sense of intimate communion into daily worship at the Tabernacle (and later, the Temple).

4.3 Affirming Holiness in Communal Life

Although the Peace Offering was celebratory, it was also deeply **holy**. The instructions about how and when to eat the meat were strict (Leviticus 7:19–21). Any ceremonial uncleanness disqualified someone from partaking in the meal, and violating these instructions could result in being cut off from the community. Thus, the Peace Offering balanced **joyful fellowship** with reverence for God's holiness.

Section 5: The Social and Theological Dimensions of Shelamim

5.1 Strengthening Community Bonds

One striking aspect of the Peace Offering is its communal meal, which naturally **enhanced social bonds** among Israelites. Family, friends, and possibly even the poor or strangers could be invited to share in the celebratory feast. Deuteronomy 12:11–12 encourages Israelites to rejoice before the Lord with their households and the Levites when bringing offerings. In such moments, **social barriers** could be eased by the unifying power of communal worship.

These meals likely fostered solidarity, mutual care, and gratitude—a foretaste of the broader vision of shalom permeating society. Through regularly gathering to eat sacrificial meals, Israelite worship helped shape a culture in which **thankfulness, dependence on God**, and **hospitality** were standard values, reinforcing covenant ideals both vertically (toward God) and horizontally (among people).

5.2 A Model for Joyful Worship

While some sacrifices may evoke solemnity or contrition, the Peace Offering primarily conveys **joyful worship** and thanksgiving. It reveals that biblical worship is not exclusively about repenting of sin; it also encourages **celebration** of God's goodness. Israel's sacrificial system thus contained a full range of emotional expressions: from lament and repentance to thanksgiving and festivity.

Modern readers can glean from the Peace Offering the biblical precedent for feasting in the presence of God, combining reverence with genuine delight. This synergy of holiness and joy appears repeatedly in the Hebrew Scriptures, seen also in Israelite feasts such as Passover, Pentecost (Weeks), and Tabernacles. The Peace Offering captures that spirit in a microcosm.

5.3 An Embodiment of Shalom

In understanding *Shelamim*, one perceives how deeply **shalom**—not just peace but also wholeness—was integrated into Israel's faith practice. By uniting worship, fellowship, and celebration, the Peace Offering provided a microcosm of **God's ideal** for human community under His rule. Such a community was meant to flourish, sharing meals and acknowledging God as the source of life and blessing.

Yet, these offerings also highlighted the reality that **true**

shalom is grounded in right relationship with God. The sprinkling of blood and the burning of fat reminded participants that divine holiness could not be overlooked. Shalom is not a casual arrangement, but a sacred state requiring covenant loyalty.

Section 6: Lasting Lessons and Contemporary Reflection

6.1 The Spiritual Principle of Fellowship

Although the Mosaic sacrificial system no longer functions in most modern faith practices, the spiritual principles behind the Peace Offering carry enduring relevance. The notion of sitting down to a meal "in God's presence" reappears in the New Testament concept of the Lord's Supper (Luke 22:14–20) and in early Christian fellowship meals (Acts 2:42–46). While the theological meanings differ, the continuity lies in the idea of **communal sharing** that acknowledges God's redemptive work.

In many Christian and Jewish traditions today, communal meals—whether liturgical feasts or simple gatherings—can serve a Peace Offering–like role: celebrating divine blessing, reinforcing unity, and expressing gratitude. The Peace Offering reminds believers that worship is not limited to private prayer or symbolic ritual but can also encompass **shared feasting** that glorifies God.

6.2 Gratitude and Celebration Amidst Holiness

The Peace Offering instructs us that gratitude, celebration, and communal happiness do not conflict with reverence for God's holiness. Modern congregations sometimes struggle to balance solemnity with rejoicing, but the Peace Offering demonstrates that **both** can coexist. Israel's community meals around the altar were festivals of thanksgiving without losing sight of the sacred.

In personal spirituality, this might translate into recognizing that times of blessing and joy are also occasions to remember God's holiness. Rather than trivializing celebration, the Peace Offering teaches that the best of feasts is enriched by a holy awareness of God's presence.

6.3 A Pattern of Peace in Turbulent Times

Another enduring dimension is the idea that Peace Offerings often followed a time of crisis, sin, or conflict. For instance, in 1 Samuel 11:14–15, after a major victory, the people and Saul offered fellowship offerings before the Lord. The pattern is clear: in moments of **relief and deliverance**, Israel turned to worship that emphasized **thanksgiving and reconciliation**.

Contemporary believers can learn that responding to crisis or resolution with sincere gratitude fosters wholeness. After enduring trials—physical, emotional, or spiritual—a "peace offering" mindset can facilitate healing, unity, and the restoration of communal well-being under God's guidance.

Conclusion

In focusing on wholeness (shalom), the Peace Offering offered a foretaste of the divine ideal for covenant community. Worshippers learned that gratitude should be immediate and heartfelt, that the best portions belong to God, that blessing is communal, and that holiness sanctifies even festive occasions. Whether giving thanks for a harvest or fulfilling a vow, the

Peace Offering was a sacred invitation to rejoice before the Lord.

Though the outward practice of *Shelamim* does not continue in contemporary worship, its principles of **shared fellowship**, **cheerful devotion**, and **celebration of God's generosity** remain profoundly relevant. Modern faith communities can still draw upon the Peace Offering's example, recognizing that true worship involves both **reverence** and **rejoicing**, that God's blessings are best honored through communal gratitude, and that every experience of deliverance or provision is an occasion to reestablish and rejoice in **shalom**. In this way, the Peace Offering endures as a potent symbol of how God intends His people to live in holistic, worshipful harmony—an anticipation of the ultimate fellowship that stretches from Israel's sacrificial altar to the final banquet envisioned in the kingdom of God.

CHAPTER 5: THE SIN OFFERING (CHATAT)

Among the various sacrifices prescribed in the Old Testament, the **Sin Offering**—or *Chatat* in Hebrew—holds a central place for addressing human wrongdoing and restoring covenant relationship with God. Although many modern readers primarily associate animal sacrifices with the forgiveness of sins, the ancient Israelite ritual system featured several categories of offerings, each with a unique purpose. The Sin Offering differs from other sacrifices in that it specifically addresses **unintentional sins** and certain kinds of ritual impurities. Through its required procedures, the Sin Offering makes clear that approaching a holy God necessitates moral and ceremonial purity.

Biblical instructions for the Sin Offering appear most explicitly in **Leviticus 4**, **Leviticus 5:1–13**, and **Leviticus 6:24–30**, setting out a detailed protocol tailored to distinct social standings and contexts. When an individual or community committed an inadvertent wrong, the *Chatat* served as the means to receive divine grace and purification. By examining the origins, procedure, and theology of the Sin Offering, we gain valuable insight into ancient Israel's view of sin and atonement—and, by extension, an important backdrop for understanding later biblical teachings on ultimate redemption.

Section 1: Biblical Context and Terminology

1.1 Scriptural Foundations

The Sin Offering emerges prominently in **Leviticus 4**, a chapter dedicated almost exclusively to its protocols. The opening instruction states, "The Lord said to Moses, 'Say to the Israelites: When anyone sins unintentionally and does what is forbidden in any of the Lord's commands...'" (Leviticus 4:1–2). This immediately sets the boundaries for the *Chatat*: it pertains to **unintentional** transgressions of divine law. Deliberate or high-handed sins generally fell outside the scope of this sacrifice (Numbers 15:30–31), indicating that certain offenses were of such gravity that the standard Sin Offering would not suffice.

Beyond Leviticus 4, subsequent passages outline further specifics. **Leviticus 5:1–13** addresses scenarios such as failing to testify, becoming defiled by contact with unclean things, or making rash oaths. These texts reinforce that "unintentional" can encompass not just ignorance of the law, but also negligence or carelessness leading to impurity or trespass. In every such case, the Sin Offering provides a channel to restore one's standing before the holy God of Israel.

1.2 The Meaning of Chatat

The Hebrew word חַטָּאת (*chatat*) is commonly translated as "sin offering." However, the same root can mean both "sin" and "sin offering," reflecting the close relationship between the act of wrongdoing and the ritual designed to address it. Moreover, *chatat* sometimes overlaps with the concept of "purification offering," highlighting that the sacrifice not only deals with guilt but also **cleanses** the individual or community from defilement. In effect, the Sin Offering is about removing barriers that sin erects between God and His people, enabling a return to covenant fellowship.

Section 2: Purpose of the Sin Offering

2.1 Atonement for Unintentional Sins

The primary function of the Sin Offering is **atonement**—*kippur* in Hebrew—for inadvertent violations of God's commandments. Leviticus 4:20, repeating a frequent refrain, declares that after the appointed rituals, "the priest shall make atonement for them, and they will be forgiven." This underscores that the Sin Offering is both **judicial** (resolving guilt) and **relational** (restoring fellowship). While it does not negate the covenant's demand for willful obedience, it does offer a **merciful provision** for times when human frailty leads to unintended transgressions.

2.2 Purification from Ritual Defilement

A second dimension of the Sin Offering is **purification** from impurity. Certain chapters in Leviticus (like Leviticus 12–15) describe how contact with bodily discharges, infectious skin diseases, or other ritual pollutants necessitates a purification process that typically culminates in a Sin Offering. Though modern readers might puzzle over why these bodily realities require ritual remediation, in ancient Israel's worldview, **holiness** and **wholeness** were intimately connected. Defilement threatened to disrupt the sacred space where God chose to dwell among His people (Leviticus 15:31). The Sin Offering thus became a key vehicle for cleansing individuals—and, symbolically, the community—from impurity.

2.3 Upholding God's Holiness

Implicit in the Sin Offering is the premise that God's **holiness** demands a response to even unintentional transgressions. The repeated emphasis in Leviticus is that the community must be a "holy people," reflecting the holiness of the God who dwells in their midst (Leviticus 11:44–45). Allowing sin or impurity to go unaddressed would undermine the covenant's integrity. Consequently, the Sin Offering serves a vital role in upholding the moral and ritual fabric of Israelite society.

Section 3: Detailed Procedure of the Sin Offering

3.1 Tiers of Responsibility

Leviticus 4 outlines a **tiered approach** to the Sin Offering, reflecting the principle that greater responsibility accompanies greater spiritual or communal authority:

1. **High Priest Sins**: If the anointed priest committed an unintentional offense, he had to bring a bull without defect (Leviticus 4:3–12). As the spiritual representative for the nation, his personal wrongdoing impacted all Israel.

2. **Whole Community Sins**: When the entire congregation fell into inadvertent sin—perhaps by collectively endorsing or engaging in forbidden activities—they likewise offered a young bull. Their priests carried out a ritual similar to that required for the high priest (Leviticus 4:13–21).

3. **Leader Sins**: A tribal chief or national leader who sinned unintentionally brought a male goat (Leviticus 4:22–26). Although not as grave as the high priest's error, a leader's wrongdoing still carried special weight due to his influence.

4. **Individual Sins**: For ordinary Israelites, the sacrifice varied. They could bring a female goat or lamb (Leviticus 4:27–35). If they were poor, they might bring two doves or pigeons or even a measure of flour (Leviticus 5:7–13). These provisions ensured that **no one** was excluded from seeking atonement based on economic status.

In each scenario, the principle is consistent: the more authority a person wields, the more serious the consequence of their sin. This tiered system reinforced accountability at every level of Israelite society, from the high priest down to the humblest citizen.

3.2 Laying On of Hands and Slaughter

Across each category, the initial act involves the sinner laying hands on the head of the sacrificial animal at the entrance to the tent of meeting (Leviticus 4:4, 4:24, 4:29). This **imposition of hands** symbolizes identification: the worshipper acknowledges that the animal stands in their place, bearing the penalty of the sin committed. The worshipper then slaughters the animal, signifying **personal involvement** in the atonement process rather than a detached or purely priestly action.

3.3 Blood Manipulation

One of the most distinctive elements of the Sin Offering is the **handling of the blood**. Whereas the Burnt Offering's blood is sprinkled around the altar, the Sin Offering's blood may be applied to specific sacred areas depending on the offender's status:

- **High Priest or Whole Community**: The priest carries some of the blood into the Holy Place, sprinkles it seven times in front of the veil (curtain) that divides the Holy Place from the Holy of Holies, and applies it to the horns of the incense altar. The remainder is poured out at the base of the bronze altar in the courtyard (Leviticus 4:5–7, 4:16–18).
- **Leader or Ordinary Individual**: The priest applies the blood to the horns of the altar of burnt offering and pours out the rest at its base (Leviticus 4:25, 4:30).

This **graduated ritual** demonstrates that a high priest's or the community's sin pollutes the sanctuary more deeply, requiring atonement even in the Holy Place. The blood, symbolizing life, has a **purifying function**, cleansing the sacred space defiled by sin. The principle is consistent: the greater the sphere of influence, the more profound the defilement, and the more extensive the blood application needed to rectify it.

3.4 Burning and Disposal of the Carcass

After the blood ritual, specific fatty portions of the animal are removed and burned on the altar, similar to other sacrifices (Leviticus 4:8–10, 4:31). For sins of the high priest or the entire community, the remainder of the bull's carcass is taken outside the camp and burned in a clean place (Leviticus 4:11–12, 4:21). This **disposal outside the camp** highlights the removal of sin and impurity from Israel's sacred center. In contrast, for individual or leader-level sin, the meat could be eaten by priests in a holy place (Leviticus 6:24–26), reflecting less severe defilement of the sanctuary.

Section 4: Distinguishing the Sin Offering from the Guilt Offering

Because both the Sin Offering (Chatat) and the Guilt Offering (Asham) address sins, it is easy to confuse them. However, the **Guilt Offering** (Asham) generally deals with **specific infractions** involving sacrilege of holy things or financial misdeeds requiring restitution (Leviticus 5:14–6:7). By contrast, the Sin Offering is broader, covering a wide range of unintentional sins and impurities without necessarily involving restitution.

For instance, if a person inadvertently used a portion of something consecrated to God, they might bring a Guilt Offering, repay what was lost plus 20%, and only then be forgiven (Leviticus 5:16). On the other hand, if a worshipper realized they had broken a commandment unwittingly or become defiled by impurity, they would bring a Sin Offering. In short, the **Guilt Offering** is typically triggered by measurable trespasses requiring compensation, whereas the **Sin Offering** addresses moral or ritual breaches that demand spiritual cleansing and atonement.

Section 5: Theological Significance of the Sin Offering

5.1 The Holiness of God and the Seriousness of Sin

Fundamentally, the Sin Offering underscores the seriousness with which the Old Testament views sin and impurity. Even if an infraction is unintentional, it still compromises the holiness of God's dwelling. The rituals surrounding the Sin Offering illustrate that **holiness is not negotiable**. To live near the divine presence, the people must remain pure. This requirement does not stem from capriciousness but from the inherent nature of a God who is morally perfect. It also reflects a **graceful provision**—God establishes a means by which broken fellowship can be restored.

5.2 Communal Dimension of Sin

The fact that the high priest's or entire community's unintentional sin demanded a more elaborate ritual clarifies another core biblical principle: **sin is rarely private**. Even unintentional wrongdoing from a leader can ripple through the community, polluting the collective spiritual environment. Such an outlook shapes how the Israelite system handles atonement: the seriousness of each offense varies with the potential impact. In turn, this fosters a heightened sense of **corporate responsibility** and mutual accountability within the covenant.

5.3 Blood as a Purifying Agent

The repeated application of blood in the Sin Offering testifies to the biblical axiom that "the life of a creature is in the blood" (Leviticus 17:11). The life-blood of the sacrificial animal is viewed as a **powerful purifier**, cleansing the tabernacle or Temple from the contamination sin creates. This is not a pagan notion that blood magically wards off evil; rather, it is a theological statement that **life—symbolized by blood—overcomes the destructive forces of sin and impurity**. The living God, who grants life, wills that sin's corrupting influence be removed through a ritually appropriate substitute.

5.4 Mercy in the Face of Human Frailty

While the Sin Offering highlights the gravity of sin, it simultaneously reveals God's merciful character. He does not cast out His people for every inadvertent misstep but provides a **clear path to restoration**. In requiring the worshipper's active participation—laying hands on the animal, confessing sin, bringing the offering—God invites repentance and engagement rather than passive guilt. The Sin Offering thus balances divine justice and compassion, demonstrating that the God of Israel is both **holy** and **willing to forgive** when approached in the manner He prescribes.

Section 6: Broader Reflections and Contemporary Relevance

6.1 Awareness of "Unintentional" Sins

One lesson that emerges from the Sin Offering is the importance of **moral vigilance**. The very existence of a ritual for unwitting wrongdoing suggests that people might sin without immediate awareness. The biblical text insists that ignorance does not automatically excuse an offense. In a modern context, this could be seen as a call to reflection and humility—recognizing that thoughtlessness, negligence, or cultural blind spots can harm others or dishonor God. By acknowledging that we do not always perceive our own failings, we become more attuned to continuous self-examination and reliance on divine grace.

6.2 Communal Integrity

The concept of corporate guilt and responsibility also resonates in today's world. While many societies emphasize individual autonomy, the Sin Offering points toward **collective accountability**. Church communities, families, and organizations can draw from this model, recognizing that leadership failures, systemic injustices, or communal complacency affect everyone. Repentance and restoration often require both **individual** and **group** action.

6.3 Recognizing God's Provision for Cleansing

Though modern faith communities typically do not practice animal sacrifice, the theological heart of the Sin Offering endures—namely, that **God provides a means** to cleanse sin and impurity, bridging the chasm between His holiness and human frailty. From a Christian perspective, this principle reaches its apex in Christ's atoning work, viewed as fulfilling and surpassing the Sin Offering's function (Hebrews 9:13–14). However, even outside a Christian lens, the Sin Offering's structure underscores the universal human need for reconciliation when wrongdoing damages our relationship with the Divine or with others.

6.4 Spiritual Discipline and Confession

Practically, the Sin Offering's emphasis on atonement through **personal engagement**—bringing the animal, laying hands on it, and confessing the sin—highlights the importance of spiritual discipline. In contemporary terms, this parallels deliberate acts of confession, restitution, and seeking forgiveness. The Old Testament's thoroughness in describing the ritual conveys that addressing sin is not a casual endeavor; it demands honesty, contrition, and commitment to restoring fellowship. Such lessons remain valuable for any faith tradition that seeks integrity in spiritual practice.

Conclusion

The Sin Offering (*Chatat*) provided ancient Israel with a structured response to unintentional wrongdoing and ritual defilement. Its inclusion in the Levitical system illuminated several core truths: **God's holiness**, the **reality of sin**, the **necessity of atonement**, and God's **gracious provision** for those who err in ignorance or carelessness. The carefully tiered regulations demonstrate that Israel's covenant community was held together by ethical accountability at every level, from high priest to ordinary individual. When the community or its leaders failed, there was a process for addressing sin, preserving the purity of the sanctuary, and restoring harmony within God's people.

Taken as a whole, *Chatat* underscores a fundamental biblical conviction: **sin, even unintentional, disrupts the life-giving relationship between God and His people**, and **atonement is necessary** to restore that bond.

CHAPTER 6: THE GUILT OFFERING (ASHAM)

Among the various sacrifices found in the Old Testament, the **Guilt Offering**—known in Hebrew as אָשָׁם (*Asham*)—addresses specific misdeeds that often involve material or relational restitution. While Israel's sacrificial system broadly aimed at preserving covenantal holiness and atoning for transgressions, the Guilt Offering has a distinct emphasis on **repaying what was violated**. Its regulations underscore an important principle: wrongdoing against God or against others can necessitate both **atonement** (through sacrifice) and **practical correction** (through restitution).

Section 1: Biblical Context and Key Passages

1.1 Leviticus 5:14–6:7

The primary Scriptural foundation for the Guilt Offering

appears in **Leviticus 5:14–6:7**, where the text addresses two main categories of offenses:

1. **Misappropriation of Holy Things (Leviticus 5:14–16)** – When a person unintentionally uses property consecrated to the Lord—such as tithes, firstfruits, or items dedicated to the sanctuary—they become guilty of sacrilege.
2. **Deceit or Fraud against One's Neighbor (Leviticus 6:1–7)** – When an individual deceives another person in a matter of deposit, pledge, robbery, or other forms of injustice, or even if they find lost property and lie about it, they incur guilt before God.

In both cases, the text prescribes bringing a ram "without defect" (Leviticus 5:15, 6:6) as a Guilt Offering. Alongside the animal sacrifice, offenders must restore what they have taken or defiled, adding **an additional 20%** (one-fifth of its value) to the principal amount. By mandating both **sacrifice** and **restitution**, the law underscores that wrongdoing has both a **spiritual** and a **practical** dimension.

1.2 Leviticus 7:1–10

Later, **Leviticus 7:1–10** describes further details regarding the disposal of the Guilt Offering. It highlights that this sacrifice, like the Sin Offering, is "most holy," and it prescribes which parts of the animal belong to the officiating priest. Much like the Sin Offering, the Guilt Offering's blood is splashed against the sides of the altar, and certain fatty portions are burned as a "pleasing aroma" to the Lord.

While these verses share similarities with other sacrificial instructions, the key difference remains the tie to **restitution**.

Thus, the Guilt Offering fills a **specific niche**: rectifying breaches of trust or misuse of sacred and personal property, and ensuring that confession of guilt is matched by tangible acts of justice.

Section 2: Core Purpose of the Guilt Offering

2.1 Addressing Sins Requiring Restitution

The Guilt Offering targets offenses in which the worshipper causes **material or financial harm**—either to God's sanctuary or to another person. This focus on tangible loss makes the Guilt Offering unique among the various sacrifices. While other offerings (such as the Sin Offering) often deal with personal or communal purity and unintentional wrongdoing, the Guilt Offering insists on **rectifying the damage** that sin inflicts in the material realm.

In ancient Israel's view, holiness was not restricted to moral or ritual dimensions alone. Economic transactions, property rights, and worship practices were all under God's governance. Violations in these areas were not trivial but threatened the sanctity and integrity of the covenant community. By requiring both sacrificial atonement and material compensation, the Guilt Offering **bound spiritual confession to ethical action**.

2.2 Demonstrating God's Holiness and Justice

A second key theme is the demonstration of **God's holiness and justice**. The Lord is not only concerned with abstract transgressions but also with how people handle what is entrusted to them—whether that is the holy vessels of the sanctuary or their neighbor's possessions. If Israel was to be a "kingdom of priests" and a "holy nation" (Exodus 19:6), it needed a system that reflected God's concern for both **vertical** (human-divine) and **horizontal** (human-human) relationships.

2.3 Restoring Fellowship

Finally, the Guilt Offering aims at **restored fellowship**. Sin, particularly when it involves property or trust, fractures relationships. By returning what was stolen or misused, the offender can mend the breach, both with the offended party and with God. The sacrifice, in turn, reopens the door to covenant communion. From the Israelite perspective, wrongdoing that alienated humans from each other also alienated them from God. Only by addressing both dimensions—repentance before God and restitution to the victim—could genuine wholeness (*shalom*) be reestablished.

Section 3: Procedure of the Guilt Offering

3.1 Identification and Confession of Guilt

The process begins with the offender recognizing or being informed of their guilt (Leviticus 5:17–18; 6:4). A critical element here is the realization that wrongdoing has occurred, whether by self-awareness or exposure. In some cases, the offender might not have initially understood the sacred status of an item they misused, while in others they might have intentionally deceived a neighbor and later felt compelled to come clean.

This **acknowledgment** and **confession** of guilt precedes the sacrifice. No offering could be made in ignorance or hypocrisy; the law was unequivocal that the worshipper must face their wrongdoing honestly. Confession included naming the offense and preparing to make the necessary restitution.

3.2 Selection of the Ram

Next, the worshipper was required to bring a **ram without defect**. A ram was considered more valuable than smaller animals like goats or birds, emphasizing the **gravity** of offenses covered by the Guilt Offering. Leviticus 6:6 specifies that the ram's value was to be measured against the "sanctuary shekel," ensuring that it met a proper standard of worth before the Lord. This costliness again indicates that wrongdoing—especially in cases of financial or property harm—could not be cheap to remedy.

3.3 Restitution Plus One-Fifth

Concurrently, the offender had to repay whatever was taken or defiled, **adding a fifth** (Leviticus 5:16, 6:5). If the sin involved misappropriating something holy (like tithes or offerings due to the Temple), the worshipper returned what they owed to the priesthood. If it involved a neighbor's property, the victim received back what had been wrongfully held, along with the additional 20%.

This stipulation ensured that the victim did not merely receive "what was stolen" but also gained compensation for the **inconvenience and violation**. It also served as a deterrent against dishonesty. Notably, the restitution element cemented the principle that spiritual atonement and ethical reparation **cannot** be separated.

3.4 Sacrifice and Blood Application

After the restitution had been arranged or made, the offender presented the ram as a sacrifice at the altar. The officiating priest performed the slaughter and handled the **blood**

application consistent with Guilt Offering protocols (Leviticus 7:2). Typically, the blood was splashed against the sides of the bronze altar, signifying the **consecration** and **atonement**.

Some texts suggest that specific fatty portions of the animal—similar to those in the Sin Offering—were burned on the altar, creating a "pleasing aroma" that symbolized acceptance by God (Leviticus 7:3–5). This ritual dimension reflected the **holiness** of the Guilt Offering. Though it addressed a wrong that had material consequences, its ultimate purpose was to restore covenant harmony with the Lord.

3.5 Priest's Portion and Disposal

In keeping with Levitical regulations, the **priest** who performed the sacrifice received a share of the Guilt Offering (Leviticus 7:7–8). Like the Sin Offering, the Guilt Offering was "most holy," meaning it had to be eaten by the priests in a consecrated space (Leviticus 7:6). The distribution of sacrificial meat to the priesthood served both practical and symbolic functions: it provided sustenance for those who ministered at the altar and reinforced the sanctity of the offering. By partaking of the offering, the priest validated the atoning efficacy of the ritual.

Section 4: Distinguishing the Guilt Offering from the Sin Offering

Although the Sin Offering (Chatat) and the Guilt Offering (Asham) both deal with sin, each has a **distinct emphasis**:

1. **Type of Wrongdoing**: The Sin Offering addresses unintentional sins or ritual impurities that demand

purification. By contrast, the Guilt Offering applies to **specific transgressions** involving tangible loss or desecration, whether of holy property or a neighbor's possessions.
2. **Restitution Requirement**: Unlike the Sin Offering, the Guilt Offering explicitly mandates **material compensation** plus an additional 20%. This stipulation underscores the Guilt Offering's role in **correcting** wrongdoing that has financial or relational repercussions.
3. **Ritual Procedure**: While both offerings involve the use of a sacrificial animal, the Guilt Offering consistently prescribes a **ram** of a certain value. The Sin Offering can vary in sacrifice according to the sinner's status (high priest, community, leader, or common person) and economic means.

In essence, the Guilt Offering focuses on the **horizontal dimension** of sin—misdeeds that result in harm to God's sacred property or another person's belongings—where rectification is indispensable.

Section 5: Theological Significance of the Guilt Offering

5.1 Divine Justice and Restoration

One crucial insight from the Guilt Offering is God's concern for **both** justice and restoration. In many ancient Near Eastern legal codes, crimes involving theft or fraud might be resolved by paying a fine to the victim. Israel's law not only integrated that practice but also **elevated it** into a sacrificial framework, insisting on an act of worship to atone for the ruptured relationship with God. Through this combination, the Guilt Offering teaches that **true justice** demands more than legal settlement—it also requires **repentance and worship** of the holy God who is offended by dishonest acts.

5.2 Holiness Extending into Everyday Transactions

The Guilt Offering highlights the conviction that **holiness** permeates all of life. Dishonesty in business, theft of property, or misuse of sacred items are not merely civil disputes; they are **sins** that disrupt the worshipping community. Israel's covenant structure did not partition "religious life" and "secular affairs" as distinct realms. Instead, it recognized that the worship of Yahweh demanded integrity in everyday dealings.

This perspective resonates in passages like Amos 8:4–6, where God condemns those who cheat the poor by falsifying weights and measures. The Guilt Offering stands as an institutional manifestation of the same principle: wrongdoing in the marketplace or the sanctuary can only be reconciled when the offender acknowledges the offense before God and compensates the injured party.

5.3 A Call to Repentance in Tangible Terms

By requiring offenders to repay stolen or misused property plus 20%, the Guilt Offering presents **repentance as a tangible act**, not merely a feeling. This principle endures in many faith traditions: genuine contrition often includes making amends. The ancient Israelite offender could not simply bring a ram, confess, and walk away with ill-gotten gains. They were compelled to correct the injustice first.

Such a standard discourages superficial confessions and fosters genuine change in behavior. In effect, the Guilt Offering demands that the worshipper take responsibility. Only then could the sacrificial portion of the rite bring the offender back into harmonious fellowship with God.

5.4 Foreshadowing Deeper Atonement

While each Levitical offering meets a particular need, taken together they paint a broader picture of **God's redemptive design**. From a Christian theological viewpoint, the Guilt Offering can be seen as foreshadowing the **sacrificial work of Jesus**, who provides both forgiveness and restoration. In the prophetic literature, Isaiah 53:10 uses the term *asham* in reference to the suffering servant—often interpreted as Christ—saying, "Yet it was the Lord's will to crush him and cause him to suffer… and though the Lord makes his life a guilt offering…".

Although this is a later theological development, it connects the principle of restitution and reparation to the ultimate redemptive act, where Jesus not only pays for sin but also brings about restored fellowship between God and humanity. The Guilt Offering thus becomes an early signpost pointing toward a comprehensive resolution for the alienation brought by sin.

Conclusion

The **Guilt Offering (*Asham*)** occupies a special niche in Israel's sacrificial system, focusing on transgressions that breach **financial trust or desecrate what is holy**. While other offerings address unintentional sins or community-wide impurity, the Guilt Offering unites **restitution** with

atonement, ensuring that confession of wrongdoing and practical redress go hand in hand. In so doing, it reinforces the biblical conviction that sin carries **real-world consequences**, and that part of seeking God's forgiveness is correcting the harm inflicted on others—whether the offended party is God Himself (via holy property) or one's neighbor.

This ancient sacrifice continues to illuminate modern faith and ethics. It testifies to a God who cares deeply about **honesty**, **repentance**, and **restoration**, holding believers accountable for the tangible impact of their actions. By linking sacrificial atonement with reparative justice, the Guilt Offering offers an enduring blueprint for addressing harm: a path where the offender acknowledges guilt, restores what was lost, and experiences divine mercy through a consecrated act of worship. Far from an archaic ritual, the principles undergirding the Guilt Offering remain profoundly relevant for communities seeking a holistic blend of **spiritual redemption** and **ethical wholeness**.

CHAPTER 7: THE RED HEIFER SACRIFICE

Throughout the Old Testament, purity and holiness stand as central themes in Israel's covenantal life. While the sacrificial system addresses many forms of sin and impurity, there is a special rite described in the Book of Numbers that deals explicitly with contamination arising from contact with the dead: the **Red Heifer Sacrifice** (Numbers 19). This ritual stands out from other offerings and sacrifices because it primarily concerns **ritual purification**, rather than atonement for moral wrongdoing. In effect, the Red Heifer Sacrifice underscores the biblical conviction that **physical mortality and human fragility** create forms of uncleanness that must be cleansed for worshippers to remain in fellowship with a holy God.

Section 1: Biblical Context and Overview

1.1 Location of Instructions: Numbers 19

The instructions for the Red Heifer Sacrifice are found in **Numbers 19**, an often-overlooked but critical chapter that addresses purification from corpse impurity. In contrast to many Levitical sacrifices, which typically took place at the entrance to the Tent of Meeting and involved priests sprinkling blood on the altar, the Red Heifer was slaughtered and burned **outside the camp** (Numbers 19:3). This difference already signals that the Red Heifer ritual addresses a unique kind of defilement and requires distinctive procedures.

Within the broader narrative of Numbers, these regulations are sandwiched between wilderness accounts and further instructions on priestly service. The emphasis on **death-related impurity** is fitting, given that the Israelites were journeying through the desert and frequently confronted with mortality. The law provided clear guidelines: for an Israelite who touched a dead body, entered a tent where someone had died, or took part in burying a relative, there was a specific remedy for restoring ritual cleanliness. Without this purification, the individual would be excluded from the community's worship.

1.2 Significance of Corpse Impurity

Old Testament law understands **death** as an ultimate symbol of impurity and separation from God, who is the source of life (Psalm 36:9). Contact with a corpse carried a high degree of ritual defilement, rendering someone unclean for a set period. Numbers 19:11–16 outlines these circumstances explicitly, specifying that those who became unclean by touching a dead body or even being in a house where someone died must be purified by the special water containing the Red Heifer's ashes.

The penalty for failing to undergo this purification was severe: the individual was effectively cut off from the congregation (Numbers 19:13).

Thus, while many of the sacrifices we've discussed in previous chapters (e.g., Burnt Offering, Sin Offering, Guilt Offering) primarily focus on **moral or covenantal infractions**, the Red Heifer Sacrifice addresses the **physical reality of death** and its symbolic pollution. This underscores a broader biblical principle: holiness in ancient Israel encompassed all aspects of life, from moral choices to the inevitable reality of mortality.

Section 2: The Heifer and Its Preparation

2.1 Qualities of the Red Heifer

Numbers 19:2 specifies that the heifer must be **red in color**, unblemished, and one "that has never been under a yoke." Being entirely red is a rare genetic occurrence, making this animal difficult to find even in ancient times. The requirement that it be free from blemish or defect aligns with the wider sacrificial principle that only the best and purest animals are offered to God (Leviticus 22:19–21). Moreover, the heifer's having "never been under a yoke" indicates it has not been used for ordinary labor, reinforcing its status as set apart and wholly dedicated to this sacred purpose.

2.2 Slaughter Outside the Camp

Unlike most sacrifices, which took place at the sanctuary, the Red Heifer was taken **outside the camp** (Numbers 19:3). The priest who oversaw the ritual—traditionally the high priest or a designated priest—would witness the slaughter but would not be the one to kill the heifer himself (the text suggests another individual performs the actual slaughter). The blood was then sprinkled toward the front of the Tent of Meeting **seven times** (Numbers 19:4), signifying completeness and sanctification. This act appears to consecrate the water to be mixed with the ashes later.

2.3 Complete Burning with Cedar, Hyssop, and Scarlet Wool

After the heifer was slaughtered, it was **completely burned** in the presence of the priest (Numbers 19:5). This total consumption by fire echoes the "whole burnt offering" motif, yet it serves a different purpose—namely, to produce ashes for the purification water. During the burning, the priest would throw **cedar wood, hyssop, and scarlet material** into the flames (Numbers 19:6). Each item carried symbolic significance:

- **Cedar Wood**: Sometimes associated with longevity and incorruptibility, cedar symbolizes strength and resistance to decay (cf. 1 Kings 4:33).
- **Hyssop**: Used frequently for purification rites (Exodus 12:22; Psalm 51:7). Its small, brush-like leaves made it suitable for sprinkling rituals, and it symbolized cleansing.
- **Scarlet Wool/Thread**: This bright red color may represent both blood and life, reinforcing the ritual's cleansing aspect.

In combining these elements with the burning of the red heifer, the ritual garnered an **intensely symbolic layering** of purification, life, and holiness, culminating in the ashes.

2.4 Collection and Storage of Ashes

Once the heifer was completely consumed, a **clean person** gathered the ashes and stored them in a **clean place** outside the camp (Numbers 19:9). These ashes would be preserved for future use, forming the essential ingredient in the "water of cleansing." Their storage indicated that the community anticipated ongoing need for purification, given the regular incidence of death in a nomadic or agrarian society. Because the ritual was so specialized, procuring enough ashes from a single red heifer could suffice the Israelite community for an extended period.

Section 3: The Purification Process

3.1 The "Water of Cleansing" (Waters of Nidah)

The essential outcome of the Red Heifer's sacrifice was the creation of a potent **purifying mixture**: the ashes of the red heifer combined with running water (Numbers 19:17). This mixture is sometimes called the "waters of separation" or "waters of nidah" in Hebrew. The text instructs that a clean person would collect some of the ashes, place them in a vessel, and pour in living (fresh) water. This water was then used to sprinkle on those who had become unclean through contact with the dead.

3.2 The Sprinkling Rite

An individual who was ritually unclean due to corpse contact had to remain in an unclean state for seven days but was sprinkled with the water of cleansing on the **third** and **seventh** days (Numbers 19:12). A clean person, using **hyssop** dipped in this water, sprinkled it on the unclean individual (Numbers 19:18). This action symbolically transferred the **cleansing power** of the red heifer's ashes, reversing the defilement caused by death.

If the person neglected to participate in this ceremony, they were cut off from Israel (Numbers 19:13, 20). The severity of this penalty underscores how seriously ancient Israel took the contagion of death—a contagion that, if ignored, threatened to degrade the sanctity of the entire community. By obeying this sprinkling rite, the unclean individual was restored to the fold, free to join again in communal worship.

3.3 A Paradox of Purification

One intriguing element in Numbers 19 is that while the water cleansed the unclean person, it simultaneously rendered the **clean person** who performed the sprinkling temporarily defiled until evening (Numbers 19:7–10, 19:21). The same substance that purified the defiled also defiled the one who handled it. Some scholars refer to this as the "Paradox of the Red Heifer," reflecting a deep sense of **mystery** and **irony** surrounding life, death, and holiness. For ancient Israel, it highlighted that **purity** and **impurity** were not merely moral concepts but states that could pass between people in the physical and ritual realm.

Section 4: Purpose and Theological Significance

4.1 Confronting the Reality of Death

At the heart of the Red Heifer ritual is an acknowledgment that **death**—the most potent symbol of human frailty—**pollutes**. Israel understood God as the ultimate source of life, so contact with a dead body, however inevitable, introduced a form of impurity that separated people from God's worship. The Red Heifer Sacrifice provided a means to overcome that separation.

This ritual element reaffirmed the biblical worldview: though death is the result of human fallenness (Genesis 3:19), God graciously offers **ways to cleanse and restore**.

4.2 Maintaining a Holy Community

The Red Heifer Sacrifice also served a **communal** purpose. In a nation journeying through wilderness camps or living in close-knit villages, death was a regular occurrence. Had there been no legal remedy for corpse impurity, large segments of the community might perpetually remain unclean. By instituting this ritual, God ensured that Israel could stay collectively **holy**, able to engage fully in festivals, sacrifices, and temple life. The repeated ceremony of sprinkling also promoted **ritual discipline**, encouraging Israelites to handle death with reverence, acknowledging its disruptive power and relying on God's instructions to mitigate it.

4.3 Symbolism of Total Cleansing

The entire process—selecting a rare red heifer, burning it entirely with cedar, hyssop, and scarlet, then using the ashes to create cleansing water—symbolizes a **thorough purification** that reached beyond everyday sin offerings or guilt offerings. This totality pointed to God's control over life, death, and renewal. The strong emphasis on **outside the camp** burning further manifested that God's holiness might extend even into spheres associated with death, conquering contamination and reinstating worshippers into communal life.

4.4 Prophetic and Eschatological Hints

In Jewish tradition, the Red Heifer sacrifice is sometimes connected to **messianic** or **eschatological** themes, as certain rabbinic sources suggest that a future red heifer will be part of end-time purification for Israel. While this belief is outside the scope of this chapter, it highlights the enduring fascination with the Red Heifer's role in cleansing from death's defilement. Some New Testament interpreters see a **foreshadowing** of Christ's ultimate victory over sin and death (Hebrews 9:13–14), where the sacrifice of Jesus "outside the gate" (Hebrews 13:12) provides a more profound, spiritual cleansing that surpasses mere ritual. Although the Red Heifer is not explicitly cited in all Christian typologies, the concept of a final, definitive remedy for death echoes in passages that speak of Christ's resurrection power (1 Corinthians 15:54–57).

Section 5: Practical and Ritual Implications in Ancient Israel

5.1 Consequences for Daily Life

Because contact with the dead was inevitable—especially in a tribal context where families tended their own sick and buried their loved ones—the Red Heifer's ashes had a **practical necessity**. Priests, Levites, or family members needed to ensure that the ashes were available and that there were individuals trained to conduct the sprinkling. This arrangement required **logistical planning**: occasional new red heifers might be found or raised, and ashes from previous sacrifices carefully guarded.

Moreover, the ritual's complexity likely fostered an atmosphere of **reverential caution** toward death. While grieving was an important part of Israelite culture (Genesis 50:10; 1 Samuel 31:13), the purification laws reminded mourners that approaching God in worship demanded rectifying any impurity from the deceased.

5.2 Maintaining a Supply of Ashes

Historically, Jewish tradition holds that only a small number of red heifers were ever sacrificed—some rabbinic sources claim as few as nine throughout Israel's history—because the ashes from a single heifer could suffice for many years. Whether this is strictly accurate or more legendary, it reflects the belief that the Red Heifer was **rare** and **precious**. The community's ability to maintain cleanliness rested on finding or nurturing these singular animals. This underscores the significance placed on continuing the ritual as part of Israel's **religious identity**.

5.3 The Role of Priests and Clean Persons

The Red Heifer ceremony blurred some lines of standard priestly function. While a priest oversaw the ritual, the actual slaughter might be performed by another individual (Numbers 19:3). Additionally, those who gathered the ashes or performed the sprinkling did so under precise conditions, highlighting that **obedience** to God's instruction was paramount. Failure to follow these details resulted in further contamination, and the law spelled out how those who participated in the ritual became temporarily unclean themselves (Numbers 19:7–8).

These stipulations created a **layered structure of holiness**: the ritual was designed to remove severe impurity, yet it also introduced a secondary defilement to the participants—clean until evening—indicating the delicate boundaries of purity in Israel's worldview.

Conclusion

Theologically, the Red Heifer stands as a testament to the Old Testament's breadth: **holiness** is not merely about moral virtue but also about **physical and ritual** states that reflect God's nature. By cleansing even the impurity of death, Yahweh demonstrated His sovereignty over the ultimate sign of human frailty. In the broader scope of Scripture, this ceremony foreshadows the hope that God's power to bring **life from death** would one day culminate in a more final, transformative act. Whether viewed in a Jewish context anticipating a future red heifer or through a Christian lens seeing Christ's triumph over the grave, the ritual resonates with the truth that **death's defilement is not final**—God provides a path toward renewed purity and fellowship, both then and now.

CHAPTER 8: THE TWO GOATS OF YOM KIPPUR (DAY OF ATONEMENT)

Among the sacred observances in ancient Israel, **Yom Kippur**—the Day of Atonement—reigns as the most solemn and significant. Held annually on the tenth day of the seventh month (Tishrei), it is a day dedicated to repentance, self-denial, and reconciliation between God and His covenant people (Leviticus 23:26–32). While the broader rituals of Yom Kippur encompass priestly garments, incense offerings, and multiple sacrifices, the highlight for many readers is the fate of the **two goats** presented before the Lord. One goat was sacrificed as a Sin Offering, and its blood was used to cleanse the Most Holy Place; the other was selected "for Azazel," symbolically carrying the sins of Israel into the wilderness (Leviticus 16:5–10).

Section 1: Scriptural Foundations in Leviticus 16

1.1 Context of Leviticus 16

The instructions for Yom Kippur appear in **Leviticus 16**, situated after the death of Aaron's two sons, Nadab and Abihu, who had offered "unauthorized fire" before the Lord (Leviticus 10:1–2). This sobering event underlines the **danger** of approaching God's holiness flippantly. Against this backdrop, Leviticus 16 delineates precisely how the high priest (initially Aaron) must enter the Holy of Holies once each year to make atonement for himself, his household, and all the assembly of Israel (Leviticus 16:2–3, 16).

1.2 Presentation of the Two Goats

Among the detailed rituals, the text calls for Aaron to take from the Israelite congregation **two male goats** as a Sin Offering (Leviticus 16:5). After sacrificing a bull for his own sin, Aaron is to cast lots over the two goats—one goat "for the Lord," and the other "for Azazel" (Leviticus 16:8). Thus, from the outset, the goats share a single offering category but will undergo divergent destinies. This division is foundational to the spiritual dynamic of Yom Kippur: one goat's blood cleanses the sanctuary, while the other goat symbolically removes the people's iniquities.

Section 2: Preparation of the High Priest

The High Priest's preparation for the Day of Atonement was critical to ensuring the success of the rituals. His cleansing, clothing, and personal atonement emphasized the holiness required for entering God's presence.

2.1. Isolation and Purity

Traditionally, the High Priest **separated himself** from the people for **seven days** before Yom Kippur. This isolation ensured he would not become ritually defiled through **contact with death or impurity** (Leviticus 21:10-12). Some traditions suggest he stayed in a special chamber within the Temple to avoid contamination.

During this time, he repeatedly reviewed the sacred rituals to ensure he performed them perfectly. He also rehearsed pronouncing the **holy name of God (YHWH)**, which was spoken only on this day.

2.2. Bathing and Changing into Sacred Garments

On the morning of Yom Kippur, the High Priest **bathed completely in water** to symbolize purification (Leviticus 16:4). Unlike the regular **golden garments** worn daily, he donned **simple white linen garments**:

- A **linen tunic (kethoneth)**
- **Linen trousers (miknesei bahd)**
- A **linen sash (avnet)**
- A **linen turban (mitznefet)**

These garments symbolized humility and purity, reflecting his role as a mediator between God and Israel (Exodus 28:39-43). He removed his high priestly gold-adorned attire because, on this day, he approached God in humility, not in kingly splendor.

2.3. Personal Atonement and Sin Offering

Before interceding for Israel, the High Priest had to **offer a**

bull as a **sin offering** for himself and his household (Leviticus 16:6). This offering demonstrated that even the High Priest was not exempt from sin and required atonement.

He laid his hands on the bull's head, **confessing his sins and those of his family** (Leviticus 16:11). This act symbolized the transfer of guilt onto the animal. Hebrews 7:27 contrasts this with Jesus, our High Priest, who was sinless and offered Himself **once for all**.

2.4. Ensuring Ritual Perfection

No one else was permitted inside the **Holy of Holies** while the High Priest performed the atonement rites (Leviticus 16:17). He bore full responsibility for Israel's atonement (Numbers 18:1). Any mistake could result in divine judgment, so the utmost care was taken in preparation.

This thorough preparation emphasized the **seriousness of approaching a holy God** and foreshadowed the perfect work of Christ in atoning for humanity.

Section 3: Offering the Bull for the High Priest's Atonement

Before making atonement for the people, the High Priest had to first make atonement for **himself and his household** (Leviticus 16:6). This involved the **sacrifice of a bull**, symbolizing the removal of his personal sins before he could mediate for others.

3.1. Selection and Presentation of the Bull

The High Priest took a **young bull** from the congregation as a

sin offering (Leviticus 16:3). This bull had to be without blemish, representing **purity and perfection** (Leviticus 4:3).

Standing at the entrance of the **Tabernacle**, he placed his hands on the bull's head and **confessed his sins and those of his household** (Leviticus 16:6). This act symbolized the **transfer of sin** from himself to the animal, preparing it to bear the penalty of sin on his behalf.

3.2. The Slaughter of the Bull

After confession, the High Priest **slaughtered the bull** as a **sin offering** for himself and his family (Leviticus 16:11). This was necessary because, as a human, he too was sinful and needed atonement before entering God's presence (Hebrews 9:7).

The **shedding of blood** was essential for atonement, as stated in **Leviticus 17:11**, "For the life of the flesh is in the blood… it is the blood that makes atonement for the soul." This foreshadowed **Jesus Christ**, who, unlike the High Priest, needed no sacrifice for Himself, as He was sinless (Hebrews 7:27).

Section 4: The Goat "for the Lord"

4.1 The Sin Offering and Ritual Significance

The goat identified "for the Lord" is sacrificed as a Sin Offering (Leviticus 16:9). Its blood, along with the bull's blood offered earlier by Aaron for his own sins, is carried into the Holy of Holies. Aaron sprinkles the goat's blood on and in front of the atonement cover (the "mercy seat") that sits atop the Ark of the Covenant (Leviticus 16:15). By doing so, the high priest makes atonement for the Most Holy Place, cleansing it from the impurities of the Israelites' transgressions.

This ritual underscores the **seriousness of sin** even for a chosen, covenant people. During the preceding year, any unintentional sins, unaddressed transgressions, and symbolic impurities accumulated in the sacred space (cf. Leviticus 16:16). The shedding and sprinkling of the goat's blood serve to **purify** God's dwelling from these pollutants, illustrating that sin's corrupting power extends beyond the individual, tainting the very place where God's presence resides among His people.

4.2 Atonement for the Sanctum and the Community

The Sin Offering goat thus emphasizes **corporate sin**—transgressions that affect the entire community. Even if individuals brought Sin Offerings throughout the year for personal wrongdoings, Yom Kippur stands as an annual reckoning, ensuring that **all** hidden or unconfessed sins are dealt with. Leviticus 16:33 summarizes this dimension: the Day of Atonement aims to cleanse the Most Holy Place, the Tent of Meeting, the altar, the priests, and all the people of Israel. This highlights an **interlocking** of holiness: the sanctity of God's priests, worship space, and covenant congregation are inseparable.

From a theological perspective, the goat's sacrificial blood addresses the **internal** aspect of guilt within the sanctuary and community. By sprinkling the altar and holy objects, the priest symbolically reclaims the sanctum for God's holiness, reaffirming the covenant bond that sin threatens to undermine.

Section 5: The Goat "for Azazel"

5.1 Understanding the Term "Azazel"

Leviticus 16:8, 10 introduces the second goat "for Azazel," a Hebrew term subject to various interpretations. Common theories include:

1. **Azazel as a Wilderness Demon**: Some scholars argue that Azazel represents a demonic entity or desert spirit. The goat is sent into the wilderness as a symbolic expulsion of sin to the "domain of evil."
2. **Azazel as "Complete Removal"**: A linguistic reading suggests "Azazel" could derive from Hebrew roots meaning "to remove," implying that this goat is the "goat of removal."
3. **Azazel as a Geographic Place**: Others propose that Azazel may refer to a rugged cliff or remote location.

Regardless of which view one adopts, the main point in Leviticus 16 is that **one goat is sent away** from the community, bearing the iniquities of Israel.

5.2 The Laying On of Hands and Confession of Sin

After sacrificing the first goat, Aaron takes the second goat and **lays both hands** on its head, confessing over it "all the wickedness and rebellion of the Israelites—all their sins" (Leviticus 16:21). This ritual gesture embodies **transfer of guilt**—the sins of the entire nation are symbolically placed upon the goat. Because Yom Kippur deals with sins that might not have been covered by individuals' offerings, this inclusive act demonstrates that even unintentional or unknown transgressions must be addressed for the community to stand guiltless before God.

The theology behind the laying on of hands is that of **identification**. In effect, the goat becomes a **sin-bearer**, carrying the burden of Israel's wrongdoing, so that the people themselves are freed from it. This function extends beyond typical Sin or Guilt Offerings, which address specific misdeeds. The Azazel goat deals with the **aggregate** of guilt—the cumulative effect of sin on the entire community.

5.3 Expulsion into the Wilderness

Once Aaron finishes confessing the sins, the goat is entrusted to a designated individual who leads it away from the camp into the wilderness, often understood as a place of **desolation** and **separation** (Leviticus 16:21–22). There, the goat is set loose, figuratively **carrying away** the sins of Israel. By removing the goat from the community's midst, the ritual dramatizes the idea that God has separated His people from their sins "as far as the east is from the west" (cf. Psalm 103:12).

This outward, **visible** demonstration adds a powerful dimension to atonement theology: while the sacrificial goat dealt with purification **within** the sanctuary, the scapegoat's departure into the wilderness illustrates a **removal** of sin from the covenant community. Hence, Yom Kippur achieves both **internal cleansing** (blood purifying the Holy Place) and **external removal** (the goat for Azazel departing with the people's iniquities).

Section 6: The Holiness of Yom Kippur

6.1 Solemn Fasting and Self-Denial

Leviticus 23:27–32 declares that on the Day of Atonement,

Israel must "afflict" or "deny" themselves, typically understood to mean **fasting** and abstaining from regular work or pleasures. This solemn atmosphere underscores the **gravity** of sin and the **urgency** of repentance. Though the two goats serve as the most dramatic visual of atonement, the entire day is immersed in a sense of introspection, humility, and sincerity before the Lord.

6.2 The High Priest's Special Role

Only on Yom Kippur did the high priest don **simple linen garments** to enter the Holy of Holies and sprinkle the sacrificial blood (Leviticus 16:4). These garments, less ornate than the usual priestly attire, reflect a posture of **repentant service**. The high priest stands as a mediator between sinful Israel and the holy God, risking his life if he fails to follow the prescribed procedures (Leviticus 16:2).

The entire chapter of Leviticus 16 emphasizes that none but the high priest can perform these rites, highlighting **hierarchical access** to the divine presence. By bridging the gap for the nation, the high priest foreshadows a greater, permanent mediation to come, a topic explored more deeply in other contexts of redemptive history.

6.3 Corporate Atonement

An essential feature of Yom Kippur is its **corporate** nature. While individual offerings throughout the year addressed personal sins, the Day of Atonement encompasses all Israel, covering unknown or unresolved trespasses. It cultivates a sense of **communal unity**, where everyone relies on the atoning power of these two goats. The focus is not simply on personal piety but on **national repentance** and the renewal of covenantal bonds.

Section 7: Symbolic and Theological Dimensions

7.1 Dual Atonement: Cleansing and Removal

By splitting the atonement process between two goats, Yom Kippur communicates a **dual dimension** of atonement: one goat's blood cleanses the sanctuary (a **vertical** dimension), while the other goat carries sin away from the people (a **horizontal** or **external** dimension). Both aspects are necessary for **complete** reconciliation with God:

1. **Purity**: The inner sanctum, tainted by sin, is purified.
2. **Expiation/Removal**: The sins themselves are expelled from the covenant community.

This twofold approach underscores how sin damages both God's dwelling place and the hearts of the people. True atonement must therefore address both the sanctuary's contamination and the people's moral burden.

7.2 The Reality of Sin and Grace

The enactment of scapegoating—transferring iniquity onto a creature removed from the camp—powerfully conveys the reality of sin's **weight** and the grace that God extends to absolve it. Rather than ignoring or downplaying wrongdoing, Yom Kippur's ritual invests it with **solemn drama**, ensuring that the community faces sin squarely. Yet, it also presents a merciful resolution: God has provided a way for the entire nation to be unburdened, year after year.

7.3 Anticipation of Perfect Atonement

In later Jewish and Christian theology, Yom Kippur often becomes a **type** or **shadow** of a greater sacrifice. The New Testament, particularly in Hebrews 9:6–14, draws parallels between the high priest's annual entrance into the Holy of Holies and the once-for-all atoning sacrifice of Jesus Christ. While the epistle does not dwell heavily on the scapegoat, it highlights that the ephemeral covering provided by Yom Kippur points forward to a more complete and enduring atonement—a subject further explored in a broader theological context, though it is only briefly mentioned here to situate the Day of Atonement within the arc of redemptive history.

Section 8: Additional Rituals and Considerations

8.1 Disposal of the Goat Handler's Garments

After leading the scapegoat into the wilderness, the person responsible for this task had to wash his clothes and bathe before re-entering the camp (Leviticus 16:26). This detail parallels the **mystery** of sin transference: though the scapegoat is removed, contact with the ritual conveys temporary impurity to the handler. Similar to the Red Heifer ritual (Numbers 19), the act of removing impurity creates a secondary form of impurity in the one performing the removal. This structural pattern reaffirms the seriousness of sin as a **contagious** or **transferable** defilement.

8.2 The Body of the Sin Offering

The remains of the bull and the goat for the Sin Offering were taken **outside the camp** and burned (Leviticus 16:27). As with certain high-level Sin Offerings, the requirement to burn the carcasses outside the camp underscores the sense that **all aspects** of defilement must be removed from God's holy dwelling (cf. Leviticus 4:12, 4:21). This action complements the scapegoat's departure, further illustrating that the camp of Israel is purged entirely of sin and impurity on Yom Kippur.

Section 9: Yom Kippur in Israel's Spiritual Life

9.1 Annual Reset

While daily offerings and other periodic sacrifices addressed ongoing spiritual issues, **Yom Kippur served as an annual "reset button."** It guaranteed that, once a year, the entire community reflected on its covenant obligations, seeking comprehensive forgiveness. By acknowledging that sin inevitably accumulates—sometimes hidden or overlooked—the Day of Atonement anchored Israel in a yearly cycle of **renewal and reconciliation**.

9.2 Communal Reflection and Repentance

The intensity of the ritual, fasting, and cessation of work on Yom Kippur encouraged deep **community reflection**. Families, tribes, and individuals collectively contemplated their moral failings, trusting that God would honor their humility. Even in post-Temple Judaism, after sacrificial rites ceased, Yom Kippur remained central as a day of prayer, fasting, and seeking forgiveness, preserving the theme of **national repentance** established in Leviticus 16.

9.3 Emphasis on God's Mercy

While the Day of Atonement is unquestionably solemn, it also centers on **divine mercy**. God provided a covenant mechanism—through the two goats—to handle the inevitable failures of His people. In an ancient context where wrongdoing against a deity could result in catastrophic punishment, this provision underscores God's character as **gracious**. The scapegoat in particular illustrates that God is willing to "cast away" the sins of His people, removing them from collective identity.

Section 10: Contemporary Reflections and Lessons

10.1 The Seriousness of Sin

Modern readers can glean from the Yom Kippur goats the principle that **sin is not merely a private matter**. In the biblical worldview, sin pollutes the community and the very space in which worship is offered. When believers recognize sin's communal repercussions, they can adopt a more **corporate** stance toward repentance, intercession, and accountability.

10.2 The Necessity of a Sacrifice and a "Sending Away"

The Day of Atonement's dual structure suggests that atonement isn't just about **purification**—it also involves **removing** guilt. Spiritual renewal requires both an **internal** cleansing of the sacred realm (our hearts, minds, and communal life) and an **external** expulsion of wrongdoing. Many religious traditions incorporate practices—like public confession or symbolic acts of release—that echo the scapegoat's function.

10.3 The Role of a Mediator

Yom Kippur spotlights the need for a **mediator**—in this case, the high priest. Humans cannot simply approach a holy God without an intermediary who follows precise instructions. This aspect invites reflection on the value of spiritual leadership, communal worship, and reverent obedience. While different faith communities express this principle in varied forms, the high priest's tasks on Yom Kippur exemplify the importance of ordered, sanctified approach to God.

10.4 Anticipating Final Redemption

For many faith traditions, particularly those within Christianity, the Day of Atonement's limitations (an annual repetition that addresses only sins committed in the preceding year) point to the hope of a **perfect sacrifice** that fully and permanently deals with sin's guilt. Even outside a Christian framework, the scapegoat narrative resonates with a **universal longing** for guilt to be transferred, removed, and forgotten. Communities still yearn for a sense that wrongdoing can be definitively dealt with, hinting at deeper eschatological or messianic expectations.

Conclusion

This yearly ritual underscores the biblical principle that God, while deeply offended by sin, graciously provides **paths of reconciliation**. The Day of Atonement thus interweaves themes of holiness, covenantal fidelity, communal unity, and divine mercy in one of the most compelling ceremonies in Scripture. Though the specifics of Yom Kippur's temple rites no longer function in the same form within Jewish or Christian practice, the core truths remain relevant: sin necessitates serious repentance, atonement requires both internal and external restoration, and God's redemptive provision stands at the center of the covenant relationship.

While other offerings in the Torah focus on personal sins, ritual impurities, and so forth, Yom Kippur unites the community in a singular act of **collective atonement**, reconciling God's people to their Creator and purging the tabernacle or temple of accumulated defilement.

CHAPTER 9: OTHER SACRIFICES AND OFFERINGS

While the major sacrifices like the Burnt Offering, Sin Offering, Guilt Offering, Grain Offering, Peace Offering, Red Heifer Sacrifice, and the special rites of Yom Kippur form the core of the Old Testament sacrificial system, Scripture also describes **other kinds of offerings** that contributed significantly to Israel's religious life and communal identity. These offerings reflect the manifold ways in which worshipers could express gratitude, devotion, and adherence to divine instructions.

Section 1: Drink Offerings

1.1 Scriptural Foundations and Practices

Often overshadowed by animal and grain sacrifices, **drink offerings** (Hebrew: *nesek*) were regular features in the life of ancient Israel. References appear in **Numbers 15:1–10, 28:7–10**, detailing how Israel was to pour wine upon the altar in conjunction with other sacrifices. The central concept is that the worshiper would present wine—generally a valued commodity—before the Lord, symbolically **pouring out** something precious as a tribute of honor and gratitude.

For instance, Numbers 15:5–7 instructs that when an Israelite presented a burnt offering or peace offering, they were also to provide a quarter hin of wine (the measure varies based on the size of the sacrifice) as a drink offering. The text clarifies that this libation was to be **poured out** on the altar, generating a sweet aroma to the Lord (Numbers 15:7). In this respect, the drink offering complemented the **savory** aspect of animal or grain offerings with a **liquid** dimension of reverence.

1.2 Symbolic Meaning

The **act of pouring** wine on the altar signaled several key elements in Israel's theology:

- **Total Devotion**: As the wine freely flowed, it evoked the idea of the worshiper's life being "poured out" in service to God (Philippians 2:17, where Paul uses similar imagery).
- **Celebration and Joy**: Wine, in the ancient Near East, was a symbol of blessing and festivity (Psalm 104:15). Offering it to the Lord acknowledged that **all joy** ultimately derives from His provision.
- **Augmentation of Other Offerings**: Most often, the drink offering did not stand alone. Instead, it enhanced animal or grain sacrifices, suggesting that worship may involve **multiple facets**—blood, grain, oil, and wine, all working together to express fullness of devotion.

In practical worship, the drink offering reminded Israel that no aspect of daily sustenance—whether grain, meat, or wine—was purely secular. Every element of life could become a **fragrant gesture of love and gratitude** to God.

1.3 Occasions for Drink Offerings

While Numbers 15 and 28 detail regular use of drink offerings alongside burnt offerings, Scripture also indicates **personal or special uses**. For example, Jacob famously poured out a drink offering when he reestablished God's covenant at Bethel (Genesis 35:14), demonstrating how this rite could mark **significant covenantal moments**. The regular practice in national worship ensured that Israel, as a nation, recognized God's sovereignty over every meal, harvest, and occasion of thanksgiving.

Section 2: Wave and Heave Offerings

2.1 Defining Wave and Heave Offerings

Among the **ritual motions** that characterized Israelite sacrifices were "waving" and "heaving," actions performed by the priest or worshiper to present certain portions of an offering to God. These ceremonial gestures are often referred to as the **wave offering** (*tenufah*) and the **heave offering** (*terumah*). While the English terms might sound unusual, they highlight physical actions used to **dedicate** or **elevate** a portion of the sacrifice.

- **Wave Offering**: Typically involved moving the portion horizontally back and forth before the altar, symbolically "presenting" it to the Lord.

- **Heave Offering**: Involved lifting or heaving the portion upward, acknowledging God's position above His people.

2.2 Scriptural Instances

Leviticus 7:30–34 and Numbers 18:8–19 describe how **portions of the peace offerings** (like the breast and right thigh of the sacrificed animal) were given as wave or heave offerings to the priest. For instance, Leviticus 7:30 instructs the worshiper to bring the breast of the peace offering as a wave offering before the Lord, and Leviticus 7:34 decrees that the breast and thigh belong to Aaron and his sons.

Another clear example appears in **Exodus 29:26–28**, where Moses consecrates Aaron and his sons. During the ordination ceremony, Moses waves the breast of a ram before the Lord as a "wave offering," and that portion becomes the priest's share. The text highlights the **transference of holiness** and **ownership**: once waved or heaved, the portion is recognized as dedicated to the priesthood by divine authorization.

2.3 Theological Purpose of Gesture

These movements carry significant theological weight:

1. **Acknowledgment of God's Ownership**: By waving or heaving the offering, the priest or worshiper symbolically declared that **God is the true recipient** of the gift.
2. **Priestly Provision**: The portion was then given to the priest, emphasizing that the priest's share was not arbitrary but **ordained** by divine instruction.

3. **Visible Participation**: The wave and heave gestures created a **physical, participatory** element in worship, underscoring that devotion required **bodily engagement**—not just mental assent.

The wave and heave offerings thus bridged the gap between the sacred realm of the altar and the practical needs of the priesthood, ensuring that the worshiper recognized both **God's supremacy** and His provision for those who served in the Tabernacle (later, the Temple).

Section 3: Firstfruits Offerings

3.1 The Concept of Firstfruits

Israel's agricultural cycles played a crucial role in shaping worship. By harvesting crops or picking produce, the people tangibly experienced God's daily provision. In response, biblical law instituted the practice of **bringing firstfruits** (Hebrew: *bikkurim*) to the Lord, a direct acknowledgment that **all produce** ultimately comes from God's bounty.

Deuteronomy 26:1–11 details the **Firstfruits Offering**: upon entering the Promised Land, Israelites were to take some of the first produce—grapes, grain, figs, pomegranates, olives, etc.—and bring them to the sanctuary. There, they would recite a short historical creed, recalling Israel's deliverance from Egypt and settlement in the land "flowing with milk and honey" (Deuteronomy 26:5–10). By presenting the first and best portion of their harvest, worshipers publicly proclaimed reliance on God's promise and generosity.

3.2 Scriptural Mandates

Numerous passages address firstfruits. **Exodus 23:19** instructs, "Bring the best of the firstfruits of your soil to the house of the Lord your God". Additionally, **Proverbs 3:9** reiterates: "Honor the Lord with your wealth, with the firstfruits of all your crops". These injunctions shaped Israel's identity as a people who recognized God's sovereignty over the land He bestowed upon them. Rather than attributing success to human effort alone, they gave **the initial yield** back to the Lord, signifying faith that He would continue to sustain the rest of the harvest.

3.3 Theological Implications

- **Thanksgiving and Trust**: By giving God the **first** part, Israelites demonstrated unwavering trust that He would ensure **subsequent abundance**.
- **Remembrance of Salvation History**: The ritual included recounting God's salvific acts, weaving the **story of the Exodus** into the yearly agricultural cycle (Deuteronomy 26:5–9).
- **Consecration of the Whole**: Symbolically, offering the first portion **sanctified** the entire harvest. In biblical thinking, dedicating the beginning of something invites God's presence over the entirety.

Even after Israel's settlement in Canaan, the firstfruits practice persisted, reminding each generation that the land was a **gift** held under covenant conditions. The principle of firstfruits extends beyond mere produce, illustrating a broader mindset: believers are to offer **the best and earliest** blessings to God, not leftovers.

Section 4: Tithe Offerings

4.1 Definition and Scope

Closely linked to the concept of firstfruits was the **tithe**—a practice in which Israelites dedicated **one-tenth** of their agricultural produce (or other forms of increase) to the Lord. The term "tithe" (Hebrew: *ma'aser*) literally means **"a tenth."** Passages like **Leviticus 27:30–33, Numbers 18:21–24**, and **Deuteronomy 14:22–29** outline how tithes were collected and used. Unlike a one-time offering, tithing operated as a **consistent** form of giving, ensuring that Israel's covenant community had **regular support** for religious and societal functions.

4.2 Purpose of the Tithe

According to **Numbers 18:21–24**, the first (or regular) tithe was allocated to the **Levites**, who lacked an inherited portion of land. By God's design, the Levites served in the sanctuary and around the tribes, relying on tithes for their sustenance. This arrangement reflected the principle that those devoting themselves to spiritual duties should share in the fruit of the land they help consecrate.

Additionally, **Deuteronomy 14:28–29** describes a **triennial tithe** (some scholars interpret it as a variation of the annual tithe) designated to assist "the Levite, the foreigner, the fatherless and the widow." This social dimension ensured that marginalized groups had provisions, reinforcing the covenant ideal of **caring for vulnerable** community members. In this sense, tithing functioned as both **priestly support** and **social welfare**.

4.3 Theological Underpinnings

- **Acknowledging God's Ownership**: By returning one-tenth of one's increase, an Israelite affirmed that God ultimately owned **all possessions**. The tithe was a tangible reminder of stewardship rather than absolute ownership.
- **Corporate Solidarity**: Tithes bound the nation together: the people provided for the Levites, and the Levites in turn maintained the sanctuary, taught the law, and blessed Israel.
- **Blessing Tied to Obedience**: Verses like **Malachi 3:10** promise that faithful tithing would open "the floodgates of heaven." This highlights a biblical theme that **covenant obedience** results in divine favor, though not mechanistically.

While modern debates about tithing vary across faith traditions, the Old Testament concept underscores God's expectation that His people **generously** support both worship and social welfare structures within their covenant community.

Section 5: Lesser-Noted and Occasional Offerings

In addition to the offerings mentioned above, the Old Testament alludes to a variety of **lesser-noted or occasional sacrifices**. Each played a particular role in expressing devotion, seeking divine favor, or fulfilling covenant obligations. Although detailed prescriptions may not appear at length, these offerings remind readers that Israel's worship life was rich, flexible, and responsive to various life situations.

5.1 Dedication Offerings

Occasionally, individuals or families brought **dedication offerings** to consecrate themselves or their possessions to God.

For instance, at the completion of the **Nazirite vow**, a worshiper presented sin offerings, burnt offerings, peace offerings, and even certain grain offerings to symbolize the end of their special devotion period (Numbers 6:13–21). While not labeled "dedication offerings" per se, these sacrifices served a **similar purpose**: marking a transition in a holy vow or vow-related commitment.

5.2 Freewill Offerings

Mentioned in various places, **freewill offerings** (related to the Hebrew concept of *nedavah*) allowed worshipers to give spontaneously beyond the mandated sacrifices. While peace offerings often covered voluntary worship, freewill offerings signaled **extra generosity** or devotion that arose from the worshiper's personal gratitude (Deuteronomy 23:23 hints at fulfilling vows or additional gifts). Although these were not required at specific times, they enriched Israel's worship with **voluntary expressions** of love for God.

5.3 Memorial Offerings

Leviticus 2:2 and 2:9 sometimes refer to a "memorial portion" of the grain offering. While this phrase specifically denotes the portion burned on the altar, the concept of a **memorial offering** occasionally appears in Scripture to suggest that God "remembers" the worshiper (Acts 10:4 uses the same idea in the New Testament regarding Cornelius's prayers and gifts). Even though this idea is not elaborated in detail for Old Testament sacrifices, it underscores that portions of offerings could function as **tangible reminders** of covenant faithfulness.

Section 6: Integration of Everyday Life and Worship

6.1 No Sacred-Secular Divide

One of the most striking aspects of these "other sacrifices and offerings" is how thoroughly they **merge** daily life with spiritual devotion. Agriculture (grain, wine, firstfruits, tithes) and typical bodily gestures (waving, heaving) become **instruments of praise** and covenant fulfillment. The biblical system left little room for a modern concept of "secular" activities disconnected from worship. Harvest time, meal preparation, or caring for the poor took on **sacred significance**.

6.2 Communal Gratitude and Responsibility

In the synergy of firstfruits, tithes, and freewill offerings, entire families and tribes learned to practice **corporate generosity**. The Levites, strangers, orphans, and widows were not afterthoughts; they lay at the heart of God's commandments for resource distribution. By embedding these commandments into the sacrificial code, Scripture wove together **religious** and **social** righteousness.

Moreover, in celebrating new harvests, worshipers realized that **their prosperity was communal** and hinged on everyone recognizing God as the source. These practices fostered **gratitude** that spilled over into **hospitality** and community-building.

Section 7: Theological Reflections and Contemporary Lessons

7.1 Holistic Worship

The lesser-known offerings underscore the breadth of **holistic worship** in the Bible. Israelites did not limit religious devotion to sin management or guilt removal. They also recognized God's gifts in **every sphere**—crops, livestock, labor, finances—and offered tokens of that recognition back to Him. Modern faith communities, too, can reclaim this **holistic** approach by dedicating not just specific "religious" times and resources but **every** dimension of life to God's glory.

7.2 Generosity and Social Justice

The tithes and firstfruits highlight a perennial biblical concern for **justice and community welfare**. While certain offerings were directed to the priesthood, others ensured provision for the vulnerable. In our own contexts, this invites reflection on how worship can be shaped to address the needs of marginalized groups. Are believers today, like ancient Israel, giving intentionally to support religious institutions as well as social ministries? The sacrificial system challenges us to consider how generosity is woven into **the fabric of faith**.

7.3 Memorial and Ongoing Commitment

The wave and heave offerings, and by extension all forms of vow and freewill offerings, underscore that worship is not static. It **memorializes** God's past faithfulness while also renewing covenant commitment. For believers today, gestures of "waving" or "heaving" might look different, but the principle remains: physical, symbolic acts—such as giving portions of income, dedicating spaces or times to God, or celebrating special occasions with worship—can **strengthen** our sense of divine-human relationship.

7.4 Continuous Dependence on God's Provision

Drink offerings and firstfruits especially illuminate the message that **all sustenance** stems from God. Even small acts like pouring out wine or dedicating the first gleanings of harvest force a worshiper to see beyond **human labor** to the Creator's blessing. In modern societies, where food supply chains and financial systems often obscure direct reliance on God, the biblical principle of **acknowledging the Giver** stands as a corrective. Adopting rhythms of gratitude—for instance, praying over meals or tithing one's income—can recapture a sense of holy dependence.

Conclusion

From these practices emerges a vision of worship that permeates **every facet** of life. Far from seeing religious duty as a narrow or isolated sphere, ancient Israel demonstrated a worldview in which the divine touches every meal, every harvest, every financial calculation, and every act of generosity. In so doing, these lesser-discussed offerings remind believers that worship is fundamentally about **relationship**—a dynamic interplay of receiving from God and giving back to Him in love, gratitude, and obedience.

For modern readers, these Old Testament sacrifices may initially seem unfamiliar or purely historical. Yet, the underlying principles—**celebration of God's provision, communal responsibility, embodied worship, and holistic stewardship**—remain potent. They challenge contemporary faith traditions to explore how to integrate worship into every dimension of existence, ensuring that **no corner** of life lies untouched by reverence for the Creator.

CHAPTER 10: THE END OF THE OLD TESTAMENT SACRIFICES

The biblical sacrificial system was central to Israel's covenant relationship with God for centuries. As we have seen in preceding chapters, sacrifices undergirded worship, atonement, communal life, and expressions of gratitude. Yet history records that **after the destruction of the Second Temple in 70 CE**, these elaborate and carefully prescribed rites effectively ceased. Without the Temple in Jerusalem, the very locus of sacrifice vanished, and Judaism underwent a profound transformation.

This chapter delves into the **historical context** that led to the cessation of Old Testament sacrifices and explores how Jewish faith communities navigated life without a functioning sacrificial altar.

Section 1: The Destruction of the Second Temple (70 CE)

1.1 Historical Background

The Second Temple period began roughly in the late sixth century BCE, after the Jewish people returned from Babylonian exile and rebuilt the Temple under leaders like Zerubbabel (Ezra 3:8–13; Haggai 2:9). Over time, this Temple became the epicenter of Jewish worship, continuing the **sacrificial practices** outlined in the Torah. Despite foreign rule by Persians, Greeks, and Romans, the sacrificial system endured, with daily offerings, festival observances, and priestly duties functioning according to biblical statutes.

Tensions in Roman-controlled Judea gradually escalated in the first century CE, culminating in the **First Jewish–Roman War (66–73 CE)**. During this conflict, the Roman general (later Emperor) Titus besieged Jerusalem. In 70 CE, the city fell, and the Romans **destroyed** the Second Temple. The Temple's holy vessels were carried away as spoils, and the once-bustling epicenter of sacrificial worship lay in ruins.

1.2 Immediate Effects on Sacrificial Worship

With no standing Temple—no **altar**, no **holy place**, no **holy of holies**—the formal sacrificial system came to an abrupt end. The daily offerings prescribed in passages like **Numbers 28–29** could no longer be performed, and the elaborate rites of major festivals like Passover, Shavuot, and Sukkot (which required pilgrimages to Jerusalem) could not proceed in their traditional form. The destruction of the sanctuary shook Jewish identity to its core, as the Temple had been the chief means of atonement, national unity, and worship.

In the aftermath, many Jews were either killed, exiled, or dispersed, accelerating the **diaspora** that had already been growing in previous centuries. Jewish leaders—rabbis and scholars—were forced to re-envision how to practice covenant faithfulness without a Temple. This event marks one of the most significant turning points in Jewish religious history.

Section 2: Prophetic and Theological Undercurrents

2.1 Prophetic Critiques of Sacrifice

While the **practical** cessation of sacrifices occurred in 70 CE, the **idea** that sacrifices alone were insufficient to secure divine favor had been voiced by Israel's prophets long before. Texts like **Hosea 6:6**, "For I desire mercy, not sacrifice, and acknowledgment of God rather than burnt offerings", and **Isaiah 1:11**, "The multitude of your sacrifices—what are they to me?", suggest that God valued **ethical living** and heartfelt devotion more than ritual sacrifice alone. Similarly, **Micah 6:6–8** questions whether thousands of rams or rivers of oil could please God if the people neglected justice, mercy, and humility.

These prophetic voices did **not** negate the sacrificial system, which was ordained in the Torah, but they **reoriented** Israel's mindset. Genuine worship required **obedience, social justice**, and **love for God**. In times of crisis, such as the Babylonian exile or the Persian period, these prophets prepared the people to realize that God's favor hinged on covenant faithfulness, not merely the ritual act of sacrificing an animal.

2.2 A Foreshadowing of Transition

Even before the Temple's final destruction, Jewish communities in the diaspora had established **synagogues** as centers of prayer and Torah study. While these did not replace the Temple's sacrificial role, they provided local sites where Jews could gather for worship. In this sense, diaspora communities were already adapting to life **beyond** direct temple access.

Biblical narratives like that of Daniel (Daniel 6:10) show exiles praying toward Jerusalem, maintaining a spiritual connection despite physical separation. The seeds of a **non-sacrificial** worship model—centered on prayer, the reading of Scripture, and moral fidelity—were thus germinating long before 70 CE. The destruction of the Temple gave impetus to these existing practices, leading to their widespread adoption in the absence of an altar.

Section 3: Emergence of Rabbinic Judaism

3.1 Yavneh and the Redefinition of Worship

After 70 CE, **Rabban Yohanan ben Zakkai**, a prominent Jewish sage, received permission from the Romans to set up a center of Torah study in **Yavneh**. This hub became the crucible for **Rabbinic Judaism**, which systematically replaced the centrality of temple-based sacrifices with **prayer, Torah observance, and acts of loving kindness**. Key rabbinic texts, eventually compiled in the **Mishnah** (around 200 CE) and the **Talmud** (3rd–5th centuries CE), debated how to maintain ritual purity, atonement, and covenant identity without the Temple.

One of the key rabbinic innovations was the assertion that **prayer**—particularly the daily Amidah prayers—could stand in for the **daily sacrifices**. Similarly, the recitation of **Torah** passages and the practice of **charity** (*tsedakah*) were emphasized as means of drawing near to God. While some prayers explicitly lament the absence of the Temple (e.g., the Mussaf service that references sacrifices), Rabbinic Judaism developed a complex and enduring structure for worship that did **not** depend on animal offerings.

3.2 Atonement Without Sacrifice

Levitical texts underscore that **blood** is central to atonement (Leviticus 17:11). However, with the Temple gone, rabbis such as Rabbi Akiva or Rabbi Yohanan ben Zakkai taught that **repentance** (*teshuvah*), **prayer**, and **good deeds** could secure divine forgiveness. **Hosea 14:2** ("Take words with you and return to the Lord... we will offer the fruit of our lips,") served as a scriptural anchor, implying that **verbal confession** and heartfelt devotion could substitute for physical offerings.

This view did not **nullify** the Torah's sacrificial laws but posited that in the current state of exile and templelessness, God accepts sincere devotion as a provisional stand-in. The Talmud often references the possibility of a **future temple**, reflecting a hope that sacrifices might resume. Meanwhile, the day-to-day reality of Rabbinic Judaism was a robust religious life anchored in study, ethics, and community obligations.

Section 4: Perspectives from the Early Christian Movement

4.1 The Temple's Destruction in Christian Thought

For early Christians, many of whom were Jewish, the destruction of the Temple also had deep implications. While

Christian belief held that Jesus' crucifixion and resurrection inaugurated a **new covenant**, the Temple's destruction affirmed for some that the **Old Covenant** sacrificial system had reached its fulfillment (Hebrews 8:13). The Epistle to the Hebrews, in particular, argues that the repeated offerings of bulls and goats could not fully remove sin, whereas Christ's self-offering was "once for all" (Hebrews 10:10–14).

Though this viewpoint diverged from Rabbinic approaches, it shared the understanding that **animal sacrifices** were no longer practiced. Christians interpreted the cessation of Temple sacrifices as **theological confirmation** that Christ had superseded the old rites with a superior form of atonement.

4.2 Christian Continuation of Jewish Traditions

Despite these theological distinctions, early Christian worship retained elements parallel to synagogue practices: reading of Scripture, communal prayer, and ethical teaching. The sacrificial dimension, however, was spiritualized in the sense that believers were encouraged to offer themselves as "living sacrifices" (Romans 12:1) and to see the Eucharist (the Lord's Supper) as the new covenant meal. For gentile Christians, who never participated in temple offerings, the question of animal sacrifice was largely moot—yet the theological significance of its cessation shaped early Christian identity.

Section 5: Lasting Effects on Jewish Worship and Identity

5.1 Prayer as Avodah Shebalev (Service of the Heart)

The Hebrew word for "worship" or "service" is **avodah**, which also denotes the sacrificial services in the Temple. After 70

CE, the rabbis referred to **prayer** as **avodah shebalev**—the "service of the heart." This conceptual leap treated prayer, especially communal prayer, as a direct replacement for the daily **morning** (*Shacharit*), **afternoon** (*Minchah*), and **evening** (*Ma'ariv*) sacrifices. The intricate structure of Jewish liturgy, including the **Amidah** prayers, was designed to correspond to the times of the daily offerings.

The result was a **dynamic, text-based** worship life. Scripture reading cycles, such as the Torah reading in synagogues, allowed communities to remain **rooted** in their sacred texts even though the Temple altar was defunct. This shift arguably **expanded** the role of **interpretation**, commentary, and oral traditions, since the focus was no longer on ritual performance at a central sanctuary but on applying biblical and rabbinic teachings to everyday life.

5.2 Continued Mourning and Messianic Hope

Jewish liturgical tradition includes prayers mourning the destruction of the Temple, especially on **Tisha B'Av** (the ninth of Av), a fast day commemorating both the First and Second Temple destructions. This **communal grief** fosters an ongoing sense of exile. Even in modern times, many orthodox Jewish prayers contain petitions for the rebuilding of the Temple and the **resumption of sacrifices** in the messianic era.

This longing underscores that, from a traditional perspective, the sacrificial system was not **obsolete** so much as **temporarily suspended**. While Rabbinic Judaism fashioned a rich, non-sacrificial practice of worship, the scriptural basis for sacrifices and the Temple's significance has never been wholly abandoned. The daily Mussaf service references these sacrifices, reinforcing an eschatological vision where, under a future Messiah, the Temple might stand again.

Section 6: Biblical Reflections on the Temple's Destruction

6.1 Lessons from the Exile Narrative

When the **First Temple** was destroyed by the Babylonians in 586 BCE, prophets like Jeremiah and Ezekiel explained that this catastrophe was divine judgment for **idolatry, social injustice**, and disregard for covenant law (Jeremiah 7:14–15; Ezekiel 8–9). The subsequent exile led to an **introspective** reevaluation of Israel's relationship with God.

Parallels can be drawn for the **Second Temple**'s destruction: the historical Josephus records infighting and moral decay among factions in Jerusalem prior to Roman assault. While not as direct as the exilic prophets, some later rabbinic texts attribute the Temple's fall to **sin'at chinam** ("baseless hatred")—indicative of moral and communal disarray. This motif underscores that **spiritual and ethical failings**, rather than mere political misfortune, triggered the loss of sacrificial worship.

6.2 The Enduring Priority of Covenant Fidelity

The destruction of the Temple and the ensuing cessation of sacrifices crystalized a scriptural theme: God values **faithful hearts** over ritual performance. Psalm 51:16–17 famously declares, "You do not delight in sacrifice, or I would bring it... My sacrifice, O God, is a broken spirit". While the end of the Old Testament sacrificial system was forced by external circumstances, it also revealed that the **covenant** could survive without an active altar—so long as the people upheld

righteousness, **mercy**, and **piety**.

This theological point resonates in both Jewish and Christian traditions. For Jews, the focus turned to an internalization of holiness, expressed through everyday commandments (**mitzvot**), study, prayer, and acts of kindness. For Christians, it confirmed a new spiritual order, interpreting Christ's self-sacrifice as the **culmination** of the sacrificial system (Hebrews 9:11–14).

Section 7: Implications for Modern Worship and Study

7.1 Cross-Faith Perspectives

The cessation of Old Testament sacrifices remains a pivotal moment that shapes modern interfaith dialogue. **Jews** view it as a tragedy but also the catalyst for Rabbinic creativity—leading to a **diaspora faith** that could thrive anywhere, no longer tied to a single sacred site. **Christians** see in it the historical juncture that validated their theological claim that the **once-for-all sacrifice** of Jesus superseded the old system. Despite differing conclusions, both traditions hold that genuine devotion transcends physical offerings.

7.2 Spiritualization and Ethical Depth

A direct outcome of losing the sacrificial system has been the **spiritualization** of worship forms. For instance, Judaism, in the absence of the altar, invests deeply in the study of **halakha** (Jewish law) and the performance of ethical commandments as a daily expression of loyalty to God. Christianity similarly encourages **spiritual sacrifices**—praise, service, and love (1 Peter 2:5). In either case, the dissolution of Temple-based rituals did not diminish religious fervor; instead, it **expanded** the ways in which believers could offer themselves to God.

7.3 The Ongoing Relevance of Sacrificial Texts

Although no physical sacrifices take place in the Jewish Temple today, the Torah's instructions on offerings remain integral to Jewish study. Traditional communities may **learn** the laws of sacrifice in the Talmudic tractates (e.g., Zevachim, Menachot), anticipating a future restoration. Similarly, Christian theologians reflect on Levitical passages to understand the **foundation** for Christ's atonement theology. Far from being obsolete, these sacrificial texts continue to shape religious thought, pointing believers toward a **holy God** who desires fellowship with His people—whether through ancient rituals or renewed spiritual commitments.

Conclusion

The cessation of Old Testament sacrifices did not transpire in a theological vacuum. In the aftermath of 70 CE, Jewish religious life refocused on prayer, Torah study, and ethical living, evolving into Rabbinic Judaism. Christians, interpreting the end of sacrifices through the lens of Jesus' ministry, found in it confirmation of a **new covenant** theology.

Across centuries, the end of Old Testament sacrifices has thus served as a **threshold**—signaling a transformation in how God's people approach Him. The violence and sorrow of the Temple's downfall eventually gave rise to vibrant new forms of devotion, bridging tradition and adaptation. Observant Jews still mourn the Temple's loss while living out robust Rabbinic faith, and Christians hold that the sacrificial imagery is perfected in Jesus' once-for-all offering. The end of the sacrificial system, therefore, does not conclude with destruction; it **unfolds** into a broader conversation on how humankind experiences the divine in changing historical landscapes.

CHAPTER 11: JESUS CHRIST – THE ULTIMATE SACRIFICE

Throughout the Old Testament, we have seen how Israel's sacrificial system operated under the Mosaic covenant: animals were brought as Burnt Offerings, Sin Offerings, Guilt Offerings, and more, each providing specific expressions of worship, thanksgiving, or atonement. These rituals saturated the life and identity of God's people, shaping how they approached a holy God in the midst of human sin and mortality. The New Testament teaches that **Jesus Christ** came as the **fulfillment and culmination** of these sacrifices, offering Himself as the final, perfect, once-for-all atonement for sin.

This has resonated for nearly two millennia, yet it remains foundational for Christian faith and theology. When first-century apostles like Paul and the author of Hebrews preached that Jesus' death and resurrection completed what the old sacrifices could only foreshadow, they rooted their conviction in the **Jewish scriptural tradition** that had long anticipated a definitive act of redemption. In this chapter, we explore how the New Testament presents Jesus as the ultimate sacrifice—an act that not only ends the need for animal offerings but also opens a path of direct communion with God.

Section 1: Jesus as the "Lamb of God"

1.1 The Lamb Imagery in Scripture

One of the most prominent titles for Jesus in the New Testament is "Lamb of God." In **John 1:29**, upon seeing Jesus approach, John the Baptist proclaims, "Behold, the Lamb of God, who takes away the sin of the world!". This evokes deep roots in the Hebrew Bible, where lambs were frequently offered in sacrifice, such as the **Passover lamb** (Exodus 12), daily burnt offerings (Exodus 29:38–39), and other communal or individual rites. By calling Jesus the "Lamb of God," the New Testament affirms that He embodies—and fulfills—the significance of these lamb sacrifices, revealing that a **person** rather than a mere animal ultimately reconciles humankind to God.

The notion of a sacrificial lamb also resonates with the concept of **innocence and purity**: lambs were to be "without blemish" (Exodus 12:5). That Jesus is depicted as sinless (2 Corinthians 5:21) accords with the Jewish requirement that sacrifices be offered from the unblemished or pure portion of a flock. This connection underlines that Jesus' sacrifice, unlike any of the repetitive Old Testament offerings, is matchless in its spotless character—He is the perfect lamb, offered once for all.

1.2 Isaiah 53 and the Suffering Servant

A pivotal Old Testament prophecy that Christians associate with Jesus' sacrificial identity is **Isaiah 53**. The prophet describes a **Suffering Servant** who "was led like a lamb to the slaughter" (Isaiah 53:7) and who "bore the sin of many" (Isaiah 53:12). Though written centuries before Christ, the early Christian community read this passage as a powerful foreshadowing of Jesus' passion and atoning death.

In Isaiah, the Servant's suffering is explicitly connected to the sins of others: "He was pierced for our transgressions, he was crushed for our iniquities" (Isaiah 53:5). This vicarious dimension parallels the function of **sin and guilt offerings** in the Levitical system, where an animal's life was given for the sake of a guilty person or community. By seeing Jesus in Isaiah 53, the New Testament highlights that what was only **typological** in the Old Testament (an animal substitute) finds its **ultimate** expression in the Messiah's self-offering for humanity.

1.3 The Baptist's Declaration (John 1:29)

John the Baptist's recognition of Jesus as the Lamb of God underscores the early Christian conviction that Jesus was not merely a moral teacher or a prophetic figure, but the **culmination** of all sacrificial imagery in Israel's heritage. When John says Jesus "takes away the sin of the world," he anticipates the global scope of atonement—no longer restricted to an Israelite sanctuary, but offered to Jew and Gentile alike.

This universal dimension of Jesus' sacrifice resonates with passages like **Romans 3:22–23**, where Paul insists that "there is no difference between Jew and Gentile," for all have sinned and all can be justified through Christ. This message, which the early apostles proclaimed, reframed centuries of sacrificial practice: the final Lamb transcends not only the daily or annual sacrifices but also the **ethnic and geographical** constraints once placed on worship in Jerusalem's Temple.

Section 2: The Cross as the Fulfillment of Old Testament Sacrifices

2.1 Continuity and Transformation

The New Testament's presentation of Jesus' death is deeply embedded in Old Testament sacrificial language. Yet it is not a simple **replacement** or duplication of any single offering; rather, Jesus' passion narrative weaves themes from the **Burnt Offering, Sin Offering, Guilt Offering,** and **Peace Offering,** among others. Each of these Old Testament types, as described in previous chapters, illuminates a specific facet of Christ's redemptive work:

1. **Burnt Offering** – Symbolizing total devotion to God, reflecting how Jesus offered His entire being—body, mind, and spirit—in obedience to the Father's will (John 6:38).
2. **Sin Offering** – Addressing human wrongdoing, paralleling Jesus' role in atoning for the sins of others (2 Corinthians 5:21).
3. **Guilt Offering** – Involving restitution, underscoring that Jesus not only reconciles humanity to God but also rectifies what sin has damaged (Colossians 1:20–22).
4. **Peace Offering** – Emphasizing fellowship, illustrating that through Jesus we have peace with God (Romans 5:1) and can partake in restored communion with Him and one another.

This kaleidoscopic view underscores that Jesus' sacrifice transcends any single category of Old Testament worship. He fulfills them all **collectively**, embodying the fullness of sacrificial meaning. As a result, the old system's partial glimpses of atonement are gathered into one **decisive** act at the cross.

2.2 Jesus as the Perfect Burnt Offering

In Old Testament tradition, the **Burnt Offering** (*Olah*) was entirely consumed by fire, signifying the worshiper's **total surrender** to God. The animal's lifeblood, representing life itself, was sprinkled around the altar, while the entire body was burnt, rising in smoke as a "pleasing aroma" (Leviticus 1:9). In the Gospels, Jesus' unwavering obedience to the Father's plan, "even unto death" (Philippians 2:8), parallels the theme of **complete submission**. On the cross, He holds nothing back—His very lifeblood is poured out, and He endures physical and spiritual agony as the supreme sign of devotion.

This analogy is particularly evident in passages like **Ephesians 5:2**, where Paul describes Christ's self-giving love as "a fragrant offering and sacrifice to God". The language intentionally alludes to the burnt offering's aroma. Jesus' self-sacrifice is not merely an accidental martyrdom but a **voluntary, all-consuming act** of worshipful surrender, pleasing to the Father.

2.3 Jesus as the True Sin and Guilt Offering

Both the **Sin Offering (Chatat)** and the **Guilt Offering (Asham)** dealt with moral and ritual wrongs, requiring the lifeblood of an animal to remove impurity and guilt (Leviticus 4–5). By analogy, the New Testament portrays Jesus as bearing human sin upon Himself, functioning as the ultimate **sin-bearer** (1 Peter 2:24). The repeated refrain in Christian tradition that Jesus "died for our sins" (1 Corinthians 15:3) indicates that His atoning death accomplishes what no repeated animal offering could—**final and comprehensive** expiation.

In **Hebrews 9:13–14**, the author makes a stark comparison: "The blood of goats and bulls... sanctify for the purification of the flesh, how much more will the blood of Christ... cleanse our conscience from dead works to serve the living God?". This rhetorical question implies that while Old Testament sacrifices dealt symbolically with sin, Jesus' death **profoundly** purifies the inner person, extending atonement to the **conscience** itself. Such a deeper cleansing underscores the heart of Christian theology: that Jesus' sacrifice addresses **not only** external or ritual impurity but the entire spiritual condition of humanity.

2.4 Peace with God Through Christ

The **Peace Offering (Shelamim)** in Leviticus 3 symbolized fellowship and communion—part of the animal was burnt, part was shared by priest and worshiper in a communal meal. In the New Testament, Paul proclaims that "we have peace with God through our Lord Jesus Christ" (Romans 5:1). The concept of "peace" (*shalom*) is comprehensive: wholeness, reconciliation, and restored relationship. Through Jesus, believers are not only forgiven of sin but also **brought into** intimate fellowship with the Triune God, partaking of a new covenant meal in the Lord's Supper (Luke 22:19–20).

This communal dimension—the idea that Jesus' sacrifice creates a **family** of reconciled worshipers—links directly to the *Shelamim* tradition. Instead of dividing the offering among priests and participants, the new covenant community shares in Christ's self-offering by faith, partaking spiritually of His "body and blood" (John 6:53–56) in a figurative sense. As a result, Jesus not only rectifies guilt but also nurtures a **lasting communion** that the old Peace Offerings only hinted at.

Section 3: The Once-for-All Sacrifice

3.1 Repetition vs. Completion

In the Old Testament, animal sacrifices repeated continually—daily, weekly, monthly, and annually (Numbers 28–29)—testifying to the **persistent** problem of human sin. By contrast, the New Testament insists that Jesus' sacrifice is **decisive** and **unrepeatable**. Hebrews 10:10 states, "We have been sanctified through the offering of the body of Jesus Christ once for all". This phrase "once for all" (Greek: *ephapax*) underscores finality and completeness.

Where priests in the old covenant "stand daily" to minister (Hebrews 10:11), Jesus has **sat down** at God's right hand, signifying the end of sacrificial labor (Hebrews 10:12). This shift from repetition to **completion** radically alters the worship paradigm: believers no longer need an ongoing system of blood sacrifices to stay in covenant. Jesus has accomplished eternal redemption in a single, transcendent event—His death and resurrection.

3.2 Perfect Priest and Perfect Sacrifice

A key argument in Hebrews is that Christ is both **High Priest** and **Sacrificial Victim**. Under the Levitical system, the priest and the offering were distinct. But in Jesus, the roles converge: He mediates the covenant even as He lays down His life

(Hebrews 9:11–14). This dual identity cements the uniqueness of Christ's ministry:

1. **Priestly Mediation**: Jesus, being sinless, enters not an earthly tabernacle but **heaven itself** to present His own blood (Hebrews 9:24).
2. **Spotless Sacrifice**: He offers not an animal but His own life, superior to any created being.

The combination of perfect priest and perfect offering means the old patterns—where human priests themselves needed atonement—are surpassed. Jesus, free from personal sin, can **fully** represent humanity before the Father, bringing about a new covenant that depends on His eternal priesthood, not on an unending lineage of flawed priests (Hebrews 7:23–28).

3.3 The Better Covenant

Jesus' atonement also anchors the **"better covenant"** prophesied in Jeremiah 31:31–34, a covenant that writes God's law on believers' hearts and grants **direct knowledge** of the Lord. Hebrews 8 applies Jeremiah's prophecy to the new covenant, arguing that by establishing a superior priesthood and offering a once-for-all sacrifice, Jesus inaugurates a relationship with God that surpasses the old. Sin is no longer "remembered" through constant sacrifices; rather, it is fundamentally dealt with, allowing worshipers to "draw near with a true heart in full assurance of faith" (Hebrews 10:22).

This new covenant dynamic fosters **intimacy** with God. Old Testament worshipers approached the sanctuary with awe and caution, mindful of the barriers around the Holy of Holies. But under Christ's high priesthood, the "curtain" is torn, symbolizing open access to God's presence (Matthew 27:51).

In place of repeated blood-shedding, spiritual worship emerges, fueled by the Holy Spirit who indwells believers (Romans 8:9–11), testifying that the once-for-all sacrifice has fundamentally **transformed** how humans relate to the divine.

Section 4: No More Need for Animal Sacrifices

4.1 The Torn Veil

A critical sign that Jesus' death ended the old sacrificial order is the **tearing of the Temple veil** at the moment He breathed His last. **Matthew 27:51** records that "the curtain of the temple was torn in two, from top to bottom," an event loaded with symbolic meaning. This curtain separated the Holy of Holies—where God's presence was most intensely manifest—from the rest of the Temple. Only the high priest, once a year on Yom Kippur, could pass beyond it.

By **tearing** this veil, the New Testament signals that Jesus' sacrifice grants direct access to God, removing the partition that kept worshipers at a distance. Not only does it abolish the requirement for an elaborate priestly ritual each year, it also announces that the **Levitical system**—centered on a physical sanctuary—has reached its culmination. The ultimate atonement has been made; the separation caused by sin is definitively breached.

4.2 The End of the Animal System

When Christians reflect on why the early Jewish-Christian community did not attempt to re-establish the old sacrificial rites, the New Testament's theology provides a clear rationale: **Christ's sacrifice is sufficient**. The author of Hebrews highlights this in repeated disclaimers that "it is impossible for the blood of bulls and goats to take away sins" (Hebrews 10:4). Rather, those offerings served as **types** or **shadows**—an educational tool preparing Israel for the ultimate remedy (Hebrews 10:1).

From this perspective, continuing animal sacrifices after Christ's crucifixion would be redundant. If the perfect offering has been made, there is no further theological justification to maintain a lesser system that pointed forward to what is now a completed reality. Thus, the Christian scriptural argument sees the old covenant as **not invalidated** but **consummated**—its purpose fulfilled and its burdens lifted.

4.3 Priesthood Redefined

The cessation of sacrifices in Christianity also redefines the notion of **priesthood**. Under Mosaic law, priests from Levi's lineage performed daily temple duties. But in the new covenant, Jesus Christ stands as the eternal High Priest (Hebrews 7:24), and all believers form a "royal priesthood" (1 Peter 2:9). This "priesthood of all believers" means worship is no longer limited to a **sacred caste** performing rituals on behalf of the people; instead, every Christian, through union with Christ, has direct access to God, offering **spiritual sacrifices** like praise, service, and compassion (1 Peter 2:5).

Hence, the end of animal sacrifices is tied to a broader transformation of worship: from a central temple cult to an **everywhere-present** spiritual service, from genealogically chosen priests to a community of believers each having a share in Christ's priestly ministry (Revelation 1:6). This theological turn is pivotal in distinguishing Christianity's approach to sacrifice from that of the old covenant.

Section 5: The Cross and Resurrection: Victory Over Sin and Death

5.1 Going Beyond Atonement

While the old covenant sacrifices primarily addressed **sin and impurity**, the New Testament contends that Jesus' work on the cross extends even further, conquering **death** itself. In 1 Corinthians 15:54–57, Paul exults that death has "been swallowed up in victory," attributing this conquest to Christ's resurrection. By rising from the dead, Jesus dismantles the ultimate consequence of sin, fulfilling the promise that new creation life is now available.

This dimension transcends the scope of older sacrifices, which never dealt directly with the problem of mortality. Indeed, the Red Heifer ritual (Numbers 19) addressed impurity from contact with death, but it did not undo death's reign. In contrast, Christ's resurrection heralds a **cosmic** shift: not only are believers forgiven, they are invited into eternal life, sealed by the power that raised Jesus. Thus, the cross-resurrection event far outstrips the old system's capabilities, offering a **holistic** redemption that affects both the moral realm and the existential plight of death.

5.2 Sin Expelled, Righteousness Imputed

Jesus' role as sacrifice also includes the concept of **substitution**. In 2 Corinthians 5:21, Paul writes, "God made him who had no sin to be sin for us, so that in him we might become the righteousness of God". This exchange echoes the scapegoat ritual of Yom Kippur, where the people's sins were symbolically placed on an animal driven into the wilderness (Leviticus 16:21–22). But whereas the scapegoat carried sin away physically, Jesus deals with it ontologically, imparting **righteousness** to believers. This imputed righteousness is a hallmark of Christian soteriology, affirming that **faith** in Christ's sacrifice brings about a real, transformative standing before God.

Section 6: The Eucharist / Lord's Supper as a New Covenant Memorial

6.1 Commemorating Jesus' Sacrifice

One might question how the new covenant memorializes Christ's once-for-all offering. In Old Testament times, worshipers regularly brought offerings to commemorate or re-experience divine acts of deliverance (e.g., the Passover recalling the Exodus). Under the new covenant, Christians celebrate the **Lord's Supper** (also known as Communion or the Eucharist) as a remembrance of Jesus' sacrifice. In **Luke 22:19–20**, Jesus instructs His disciples at the Last Supper, "Do this in remembrance of me," connecting the meal to His impending death.

Unlike the repeated blood sacrifices of the old covenant, the Eucharist does not involve **slaughter** or **bloodshed**. Instead, it uses **bread and wine** as symbols of Christ's body and blood, given for the forgiveness of sins (Matthew 26:26–28). This shift underscores that Jesus' death was singular and unrepeatable, while the **memorial** continues as a living practice that unites believers to the benefits of His self-offering.

6.2 The Bread and the Cup

Christians debate the exact nature of Christ's presence in the

Eucharist—some traditions affirm a mystical transformation (Transubstantiation or Real Presence), others a symbolic presence—but all generally agree that the bread and cup signify Jesus' sacrifice. This meal thus:

1. **Recalls** His atoning death.
2. **Announces** ongoing fellowship in the new covenant community.
3. **Anticipates** the messianic banquet at the end of the age (1 Corinthians 11:26).

In this manner, the Lord's Supper parallels Old Testament feasts that commemorated God's salvation events (such as the Passover). However, the difference is that no **new** sacrificial act is performed; participants simply receive from the completed work of Christ. It is a sacrament or ordinance that **re-presents** the historical sacrifice rather than re-enacts it.

6.3 The New Covenant Memorial vs. Ongoing Sacrifices

By instituting this memorial, Jesus provided a mode of worship that does not revert to **animal sacrifice** but still upholds the biblical principle of "remembering" divine deliverance. The continuity from Passover to the Lord's Supper is striking: in both cases, participants share a meal commemorating salvation (Exodus from Egypt vs. exodus from sin and death), but the culminating sacrifice is no longer a lamb slaughtered yearly. Instead, it is the Lamb of God—**Jesus**—once sacrificed, forever triumphant. This theological pivot reaffirms that the old system's repetition has been superseded by a **single**, definitive event.

Section 7: Ongoing Implications for Christian Life and Worship

7.1 Living Sacrifices

One of the most direct applications of Christ's ultimate sacrifice to Christian ethics appears in **Romans 12:1**, where Paul exhorts believers to "offer your bodies as a living sacrifice, holy and pleasing to God—this is your true and proper worship". Here, Paul uses sacrificial language to describe the believer's response to the gospel. While animal sacrifices are no longer required, the principle of **wholehearted devotion** endures. Christians are called to yield their lives—thoughts, actions, ambitions—to God's service in gratitude for Christ's redeeming work.

This concept of "living sacrifice" echoes the Old Testament's emphasis on **holiness**, reminding the faithful that the moral and spiritual demands of God persist. Christ's once-for-all offering does not abolish the call to purity but **empowers** believers to live righteously, fueled by the Holy Spirit rather than legal obligation (Galatians 5:16–25). The result is a community shaped by sacrificial love, echoing Jesus' own example (John 13:34–35).

7.2 Forgiveness and Reconciliation

Because Christ's sacrifice deals comprehensively with sin, Christian teaching insists that believers should exhibit a **forgiving** and **reconciling** spirit. "Be kind to one another, tenderhearted, forgiving one another, as God in Christ forgave you," writes Paul in **Ephesians 4:32**. This imperative flows directly from the notion that if one's own debt has been cleared by Jesus' supreme offering, one must show the same grace to others. This ethic underpins Christian community life, distinguishing it from a constant cycle of retribution or guilt.

7.3 Access to God and Priestly Ministry

Another practical consequence is **direct access** to God's presence. Hebrews 4:16 encourages believers to "approach God's throne of grace with confidence," an unthinkable privilege under the old covenant, where approaching the Holy of Holies risked immediate death if done incorrectly (Leviticus 16:2). The reason for this boldness is Christ's high-priestly intercession (Hebrews 7:25). Equally, Christians regard themselves as a "priesthood" (1 Peter 2:9), implying responsibility to pray for others, offer spiritual sacrifices of praise, and represent God's holiness in the world.

7.4 A Model of Self-Giving Love

Finally, Jesus' sacrifice serves as the **paradigm** for Christian love. Just as the old covenant sacrifices demanded **costly** offerings, the new covenant ethic calls for **self-giving** akin to Jesus' surrender on the cross (John 15:12–13). In families, churches, and society at large, the faithful are exhorted to "walk in love, just as Christ also loved you and gave Himself up for us" (Ephesians 5:2). This posture transforms sacrifice from a **ritual** act into a **lifestyle** of compassion, humility, and service.

Conclusion

The Old Testament sacrificial system, with its multifaceted offerings for sin, thanksgiving, fellowship, and ritual purity, established an enduring testament to the gravity of sin and the necessity of a **mediating** offering. Over centuries, Israel learned that **blood** was central to atonement, that repeated sacrifices pointed to ongoing human frailty, and that the promise of a deeper redemption loomed in the background of its rituals. In the fullness of time, the New Testament proclaims, **Jesus Christ** appeared to fulfill and surpass these symbols, becoming the **Lamb of God** who bears the sins of the world.

In examining Jesus as the ultimate sacrifice, we see how He unites the significance of each Old Testament offering: He fully surrenders in obedience (Burnt Offering), takes upon Himself the sins of humanity (Sin Offering), reconciles what was broken by sin (Guilt Offering), and restores believers to peace and fellowship with God (Peace Offering). This integrative approach attests that His cross stands at the **center** of redemptive history, bridging the old covenant's shadows and the new covenant's glorious reality.

No longer are believers bound to a cycle of animal offerings. The **veil** is torn, the "once-for-all" sacrifice is accomplished, and the need for repetition has passed. Prayer, worship, and service are now offered in **gratitude** for Christ's perfect atonement, not as a perpetual attempt to assuage guilt. The Christian life, then, becomes an ongoing response to this profound gift—a "living sacrifice" shaped by love, purity, and the Holy Spirit's indwelling presence.

Thus, Jesus' atonement does not merely overshadow the old sacrifices; it **expands** and **transforms** their central message into a cosmic declaration that sin and death have been defeated. By faith in Christ, believers partake of a new covenant that extends beyond the confines of any single earthly altar or sanctuary, embracing all nations in God's invitation to redemption. Indeed, in the cross and resurrection, the story of sacrifice finds its **ultimate fulfillment**—one that continues to inspire devotion, shape ethics, and define Christian identity for generations to come.

www.ingramcontent.com/pod-product-compliance
Lightning Source LLC
Chambersburg PA
CBHW060325050426
42449CB00011B/2660